Policem

Harry Col
Bermondse
when he w
became a c
mason and, in 1952, a policeman. For thirty years, until his retirement in 1983, he served at the same police station in London.

He is a qualified FA coach (he has run numerous junior football teams), a referee and a keen cricketer. For many years he had a regular column in the *Warren*, the police magazine. His other books are *Policeman's Lot, Policeman's Patch, Policeman's Patrol, Policeman's Prelude, Policeman's Progress* and *Policeman's Story*, his two-volume autobiography, *Policeman's Gazette* and *The Blue Apprentices*, a novel.

In 1978 Harry Cole was awarded the British Empire Medal for voluntary work. Since leaving the force, in addition to writing he has taken up after-dinner speaking.

Policeman's Travels

Harry Cole

FONTANA/Collins

To Stella Leighton, for her dedication

First published in 1990 by Fontana Paperbacks
8 Grafton Street, London W1X 3LA

Printed and bound in Great Britain by
William Collins Sons & Co. Ltd., Glasgow

Contents

A Bit of a Saga

'I'm sorry, but I'm definitely not tying them on. There is no way those labels are going to even touch those suitcases until we actually check in at Heathrow. That's final.'

'Oh don't be so vain,' reproached Joan. 'I thought it was only women who were supposed to be sensitive about their age.'

'I'm not the least bit sensitive – and I'm certainly not vain,' I protested huffily. 'But the fact is I'm fifty-six years of age. Therefore I refuse to hump two hulking great suitcases across the entire width of London that proclaim to the world I'm sixty.'

She shook her head in despair. 'But you *are* vain. You haven't heard me complaining and I'm younger than you.'

'Quite – and if I could walk three yards behind you, whilst you humped the bloody cases, you wouldn't hear me complaining either. But the fact remains you don't – so I won't. It'll be me carrying the cases. It'll be me looking sixty. So it's me refusing to flash the labels. Fair?'

'Oh come on,' she chided. 'Just how many people do you think actually *know* SAGA is an over-sixties travel club . . . and what's more to the point, how many even care?'

'*I* know and *I* care – and I'm still not tying on the damned labels. Now,' I added, punctuating each word with a firm shoulder prod, 'if you want the labels on the cases, then that's fine by me. All you now have to do is carry them.'

This whole debate had taken place as a curtain-raiser to our annual holiday. After reading an ad in my retirement association newsletter, I had booked a 'West Coast USA' tour with the travel firm SAGA. Just weeks before our departure date, I was appalled to discover SAGA was an *over-sixties* travel club.

Panic-stricken, I had raced to the telephone. 'There's been a mistake,' I had blurted. 'I'm nowhere near sixty, and nor is my wife. I'm a stripling of fifty-six and young for my age.' I had then begun to gabble. 'Can't go . . . honest mistake . . . money back?'

'Don't worry, sir, don't worry,' soothed the female voice at the other end. 'It's all quite in order. If you are a member of a retirement association, you are eligible for SAGA.'

I was not convinced. I did not want to be 'Eligible for SAGA'. It sounded like an admission interview for a geriatric unit. I replaced the receiver and gravely broke the news.

'Great!' Joan responded. 'So we can go after all!'

'Of course not,' I snorted. 'We certainly can't go now.'

'Why ever not?'

'It's obvious, I should think.'

'Well it's certainly *not* obvious to me. Why can't we go?'

'Look, there is going to be a coach full of people on this tour, right?' She nodded. 'Well, you can bet a fair proportion will be . . . well, you know.'

'No I don't know, you tell me. What *will* they be? Lepers? PLO reps? . . . Oh, of course, I've got it! They'll be double-glazing salesmen, won't they? They'll spend the entire fortnight telling us our frames are rotten. I should think that could be quite a worry.'

'Look, double-glazing salesmen they could *possibly* be. But what they will *certainly* be is over sixty,' I pointed out irritably. 'And it's just possible that the odd one could be senile as well.'

She stared at me in disbelief. 'But the tour is to California, for Pete's sake! No senile geriatric is going to undertake a tour like that.'

'I know, I know.' I perked up considerably, believing I was finally getting through. 'That's just my point. If a person *was* senile, they wouldn't *know* California was six thousand miles away. They'd probably think it was near Bognor or somewhere. In any case, even the vaguest of geriatrics would realize he wasn't going by wagon train . . . I gather SAGA does fly?'

There was silence. Conversation had reached an impasse.

Now, three weeks later, we had reached decision day. Our plane was due to leave Heathrow in a few hours and a friend was arriving at any moment to transport us in her car. We had washed, packed and cancelled the milk, but were still in disagreement over the blasted labels.

'Look,' said Joan soothingly, 'I wasn't going to tell you this. But if I didn't . . .' She gave an exaggerated sigh. 'Well, you'd probably take it personally.'

'I know, don't tell me,' I cried facetiously, 'you're going on your own?'

'You should be so lucky!' she exclaimed. 'Look, I'll tell you what. I'll make a deal with you. You tie the labels on the cases and I'll give you a vital piece of information. Yes?'

'Oh no! You tell me what it is first.'

'Well, you know you've packed everything for your holiday?'

'Yes.'

'And you know that all we are waiting for is Mary to come and collect us?'

'Yes! Yes! Yes! Get to the point, woman.'

'It is just that your case is *downstairs*, in the hall, but three pairs of your shoes are *upstairs*, piled up on your pillow.' I groaned. I had laid out everything I had intended to pack on the bed before transferring it to my suitcase. Yet I had still overlooked one pair of cream moccasins, one pair of black lace-ups and one pair of heavy brown brogues. 'I don't know why you take so many shoes on holiday in the first place,' she continued. 'I mean, it's not as if you wear them is it? For two weeks you'll do everything but sleep in those rotten trainers. Besides, you've no business putting shoes on pillows. It's unhygienic, to say the least.'

'Bugger! Bugger! Bugger!' I responded, as I plodded back up the stairs. 'I know that if I put as much as another bloody toothbrush in that case it'll disintegrate – and that's assuming I could possibly get it shut again.'

She followed me up the stairs. 'Oh come now,' she soothed, as if encouraging a six-year-old half-wit. 'I'm sure that with a little systematic repacking, you'll probably find plenty of room to spare.'

'Listen!' snarled the half-wit. 'Not only have you filled your *own* suitcase, but half of what I shall be humping around in *mine* – is *yours*! If by some miracle I could find any room to spare, then it would only be spare until you filled it with another three frocks!'

'Not *frocks*, dear, *dresses*,' she corrected. '*Dresses* is the word you want. I haven't worn frocks since I left Sunday school.'

As I began the usual wearisome task of unpacking my suitcase, I dispensed quickly with the brown brogues and black lace-ups. 'You should thank your lucky stars I'm not a transvestite,' I muttered. 'Then you really would have problems.'

'Oh, I don't know,' she said thoughtfully. 'It might even be easier . . . perhaps we could share.'

I squeezed three handkerchiefs, two pairs of underpants and one sock into each cream moccasin and wondered why I underwent this now regular travel torture. I mean, no one makes us do it. It is entirely voluntary. Yet in the weeks preceding these travels, I am at the pinnacle of scruffiness. Every decent article of clothing is either in the wash, at the cleaners, or needing a button. For at least five days I am so disgustingly awful that I could pass for a moderately successful pop star. I thrust, pressed, leaned and cursed and finally managed to close the thing. I turned to Joan threateningly; '. . . and if you tell me the passports are in the bottom, we're not going.'

'You can relax. I have the passports in my handbag, but it's your side of the bargain now.' She held out the two offending labels. 'Mary will be here soon. Are you going to be a nice lad and tie these on, or leave them off and be a vain old sod?'

If she had been in with any chance before, she had none at all once she mentioned Mary. Both Mary and her husband Dave had been making envious noises for weeks.

They had obviously thought we were undertaking some grand solo trip. I was not going to disillusion them now.

'I am not tying them on.'

'So what is Mary going to think when you put the cases in the car without labels?'

I shrugged with false indifference. 'I don't care *what* Mary thinks,' I lied. 'I daresay she'll think it's some exclusive tour we're undertaking.'

'A tour where you don't need labels, eh?' she murmured thoughtfully. 'Where do you think she'll assume we're going – Sainsbury's?'

'Listen,' I snapped. 'Mary's more excited about this tour than we are and she's not on it. I tell you she won't even notice there are no labels.'

Shaking her head, she gave a long patient sigh. 'All right, just as you wish. But I think the whole thing is childish.'

'Now there's a twist! Two minutes ago you implied I was a vain old sod – now I'm childish!'

She placed a placating arm over my shoulder. 'Vain you may be . . . old? . . . we . . . e . . . ell, possibly. Sod? Never.'

'Uh-huh, and that's supposed to make it all better is – ' further conversation was interrupted by a friendly double toot from outside.

Mary breezed enthusiastically up our garden path. 'Oh, you are so lucky to be going to California, you know. I wish I was going.' She stared down at the waiting cases. 'Where are your labels?'

Joan pursed her lips and stared aggravatingly skyward.

'It's a security measure suggested by the Neighbourhood Watch co-ordinator,' I lied.

She looked briefly puzzled. 'But your cases won't be in the neighbourhood.'

'Okay, okay. So they'll be in someone else's neighbourhood. Now can we get going? We have a rush-hour trip across London and time is cracking on.'

'Handle him carefully Mary,' whispered Joan, slipping into her coat. 'He's a little sensitive this morning. Belated male menopause, most likely.'

'Needs a holiday, I shouldn't wonder,' nodded Mary wisely. 'The rest will do him good.'

I refused to rise to the bait and seized the handles of both suitcases. Full though mine was, it was still comparatively light. Joan's, on the other hand, almost tore off my arm. Why is it, I wondered, that if a woman's clothing is frilly and light, her suitcase is always three times heavier than a man's?

I wheeled around suspiciously. 'Have you put anything in this case since I carried it into the hall?'

''Course not,' she protested indignantly. 'Well . . . just a little footwear and – er, a couple of other bits and pieces.'

'Such as?'

'Such as sun-oil and deodorant.'

'*Just* footwear, oil and deodorant?'

'Uh-huh.'

'Definitely nothing else?'

'Definitely nothing else,' she confirmed.

'Then you must have diving boots, a bucket of oil and half a ton of deodorant because this bloody thing is all but immovable.'

Mary bent down and with maddeningly little effort, lifted the offending case. 'You really do need this holiday, don't you love?' she tutted. 'Poor old sod.'

*

An hour or so later, Mary braked to a halt outside the Embankment station. Our plan was to travel to Heathrow by underground train in order to avoid the frustrations of a road journey.

'You'd better fix your labels on now,' she advised. 'Those trains can be so packed you can lose anything on them.'

'Anything except Joan's case,' I pointed out. 'They'd have to lift it first.'

'I wasn't speaking of the cases,' she explained, 'I was thinking of the labels. What with tickets, passports and all the other bits and pieces, I thought you'd be better tying them on now.'

'Er – no. I don't think so, Mary. In fact the Neighbourhood Watch co-ordinator was quite insistent on that very point. "What ever you do," he said, "Don't put your labels on until the last possible minute." I do really feel that's sound advice, you know.'

'I'm sure it is,' she answered drily. 'In fact, if you didn't put them on at all, no one would know you'd been away. Here, that's a point,' she added, her eyes narrowing. 'I suppose you are *going* to California? I mean, you've not been kidding me all along and going to Cleethorpes or somewhere are you?'

'Well that's nice, I must say – Cleethorpes! Why'd you think of that?'

She shrugged. 'Well it does seem that you haven't any labels – and you wouldn't need them for Cleethorpes, would you? Just a certificate of sanity would do. Anyway, Cleethorpes or California, have a really great time and send us a card.'

The minute it took to remove our cases from the boot of that little Vauxhall seemed to block the Victoria

Embankment halfway to south Wales. Leaving Mary to make her peace with three buses, two taxis and a distant traffic warden, we hastened into the depths of the District line.

'I don't think that was particularly gallant of you, to dash away and leave the girl like that,' reproved Joan.

'I can hardly "dash away" as you put it, with your case. Anyway, she'll manage,' I assured her. 'By the time she's demanded to see all their labels and badges, they'll be only too pleased to be rid of her.'

Having pointed out to Joan that merely lifting her suitcase should absolve me from purchasing tickets, I took a much-needed breather whilst she queued at the kiosk. On the ride down the escalator, I studied the ladies' underwear advertisements more thoughtfully than usual. I am sure that women never look at these pictures. One only has to see the turning heads to realize that. Previously though, I had put my enthusiasm down to a healthy, biological interest in the opposite sex. Nothing wrong there, I would claim. However, as I was then embarking on my first SAGA tour, was I now, I wondered, a dirty old man? I made a mental note to buy dark glasses.

The rest of the UK assume that Londoners have it made when it comes to travelling to the two large international airports at Gatwick and Heathrow. If only they knew!

Take Gatwick, for example. It proudly boasts a thirty-minute express train journey from Victoria station that will transport you practically on to your plane. Great! 'Great' that is, if you *live* in Victoria. But except for the Queen – and it has been a year or two since *she* went on a package tour – no one does. Do you know anyone who lives in Victoria? Because although they now claim I am eligible for SAGA, I have never met anyone who even lives near the place.

This express train service they brag so much about goes non-stop and rocket-like along the elevated line that skims the south London roof-tops. It is usually half full of happy north-country holidaymakers, wallowing in the spaciousness. Meanwhile, at street level, masses of Gatwick-bound Londoners struggle manfully as they endeavour to wedge their thirty-one-inch suitcases into the twenty-six-inch recesses that suffice on the average London Transport omnibus.

A couple of years ago, on a solo journey and China-bound, I had probably complained even more strongly than usual. Joan, rather unkindly I thought, accused me of being spoilt. (Me! Who spent the first eight holidays of his life hop-picking!)

'Here you are,' she remonstrated, 'And all you have to do is get yourself across London to the airport. Anyone would think it an insurmountable task. Within twenty-four hours, you'll be in Peking. Don't you know that Mao Tse-Tung *walked* across the whole width of China without so much as a complaint? He said something which you would do well to bear in mind.'

'Oh yeh, and that was?'

'He said, "The journey of a thousand miles begins with the first step." Doesn't that make you feel ashamed?'

'Not a bit. All he had to do was walk across China. That's easy, any fool could do that. I've got to bloody *fly* there. My journey doesn't begin with "one step" at all. It begins with that rotten trip to Heathrow. I may well have a nine-thousand-mile journey ahead of me but when I finally reach London Airport, I will consider I've cracked it.'

'But you can go all the way to Heathrow by underground train now,' she pointed out.

Now this statement just proved to me how the public at large had been hoodwinked by London Transport's publicity campaign on the alleged ease of travel to Heathrow. Take the station I was on at that moment – the Embankment. The west-bound traveller sees a west-bound train and naturally assumes he is in luck. First mistake.

District line trains from the Embankment race away purposefully but then seem to lose interest around Earls Court and meander off into assorted directions. Not that I blame anyone for that. I was in the army for a time near Hounslow, and anyone who avoids the place and squiggles off to Kew Gardens has my complete understanding. Now nice though this detour may be, it is a little hard on a jet-setting China-bound smoothie, humping his compressed cardboard case towards the three o'clock flight to Peking.

An additional hazard is train-changing. The passenger can be on the correct train, be on the correct line, even at the correct time but you can safely bet your passport on a loud 'ALL CHANGE PLEASE!' from the guard, who is never seen on any other occasion. Regular travellers to Heathrow know that ninety per cent of all London Transport trains go to a place called Turnham Green. No one appears to know why this is. I was so intrigued by this phenomenon that I once went to Turnham Green to see for myself. I found nothing to interest the casual traveller. If anything, it is more boring than Victoria. Yet London Transport obsessively believe that three-quarters of their travelling public wish to be deposited there. I can only assume it is the west London equivalent of a pilgrimage to Mecca. Once you have been there you can probably paint your house a different colour and wear a wider belt on your kaftan.

Finally comes the last hurdle before the traveller's triumphant arrival at the airport proper. This is something in the nature of a joke. It is called (to the fiendish amusement of the comedian who designed it) 'Terminal Four Underground Station'. For the unwary, this is the moment they begin to relax in the fatuous belief that the first part of their journey is complete. Not so. In fact, the word 'terminal' could well prove to be apt. All that has happened is that the trusting traveller has been deposited at a location that displays a sign claiming to be 'Terminal Four'. During the next thirty minutes' walk (there will be no vacant trolleys), it will be universally agreed that the sign could have as easily read Plymouth, or Nore Lightship, both locations seemingly marginally closer.

The automatic doors at last swing open and there it is in all its horrendous glory – 'London Airport Terminal Four Check-in'. You crawl in on your knees, elated that your journey has at last begun. Stanley found Livingstone more easily.

It was on this journey to the airport that Joan once more, and at last successfully, implored me to tie on the labels.

'Look,' she pleaded, 'we've survived Turnham Green, we're still on the train and the bears haven't eaten us. Now will you fix on those rotten labels?'

Her point was reinforced by our travelling companions. Just a few seats away sat two couples, obviously travelling as a foursome. They were smartly dressed, lively, and considering their ages – around sixty-five I guessed – quite good-looking. Joan tugged my sleeve and leaned her head towards me. I offered an ear.

'See that foursome?' she whispered.

'Yes.'

'Smart group, eh?'

I nodded.

'See their labels? . . . on those cases by the door.'

I turned towards four expensive pieces of beige leather stacked at the end of the row of seats. Proudly displayed on each was a large label with the word SAGA emblazoned in capitals.

'Impressed, eh?' she hissed.

It would have been churlish to have denied it. I was impressed. The quartet looked wholesome enough for laxative commercials. I nodded a grudging agreement.

'So you wouldn't mind a fortnight with a coachload of them?' she persisted.

'Well . . . yes,' I conceded, 'but let's not get *too* carried away. I mean, once you get to know them they may be quite boring. Then two weeks can be a helluva time.'

'Oh, I shouldn't think you'd have any worry on that count,' she whispered, warming to her self-appointed task. 'Look at them closely. They have clean, bright, joyful faces. You don't even get that sort of serenity at a Billy Graham meeting. They look for all the world like four big, happy, innocent puppies.'

I thought this was way over the top, particularly as the nearest she had ever been to Billy Graham was Sammy Davis doing an impression of him. Yet funnily enough, I could see what she meant. They were all gently rounded and seemed happy to the point of playfulness in each other's company. With their light fawn padded coats and their blond to white hair, they reminded me of golden retrievers. Although I did not share all her enthusiasm, I had to admit it was the most promising of starts.

At the entrance to the Terminal Hall, I dropped my cases to look for the longest queue. Experience of package tours has taught me that, Jersey or Japan, if you are with a tour company, your queue will be the longest in the building. The search was a pushover. There was only one line in sight that sported more than six people. It was the one where some fifty-odd SAGA-labelled people stood patiently, if not silently, in a long, crooked squiggle. I slid the cases to the heels of the last person in the line and exhaustedly sat down upon them.

'You realize that if anything happened to me you'd never go on holiday again, I s'pose,' I panted.

'Why ever not?' she asked.

'Because no other idiot would carry your suitcase. Do you know that after thirty years of holidays with you my left arm is so developed I could swing non-stop across Borneo? You've made me a freak, d'you know that? My right shoulder is as delicate as Dresden china and my left looks like Arnold Schwarzenegger's.'

The years that had given me this buffalo shoulder had also taught me something else; that at moments like this, Joan will always change the subject. She was on cue to the instant.

'Hey!' she whispered. 'How about her! She's never a SAGA client, surely.'

Although I was expecting the ploy, I was definitely not expecting the subject. I have to admit that even at that early stage, I was intrigued. Meanwhile, the laxative-commercial quartet eased smoothly in behind us.

The reason for Joan's doubt was an obvious one. It concerned the appearance of the female traveller immediately to our front. The woman had a large SAGA label on her suitcase, plus another on her hand luggage. She also had a self-adhesive sticker on her collapsible umbrella, plus two more on her handbag. In other words, an over-sixty SAGA traveller if ever there was one. Yet these adornments seemed totally contradicted by her rear view, the most notable feature of this being a mass of flame-red hair that cascaded down her green, skin-tight velour trouser-suit, reaching the small of her back. Her pants were so dangerously stretched across her rounded buttocks that an outline of the washing instructions could be seen, protruding from the top of her minuscule briefs.

These buttocks only reluctantly tapered into plump, over-generous thighs, which in turn only grudgingly gave up their bulk to the powerful muscles of her lower limbs. All this incredibly stacked womanhood tottered alarmingly on two extremely high-heeled, sling-backed, luminous-green sandals. It was truly a superb feat of balance. As I marvelled, my attention was drawn to the crimson-nailed fingers of the hand that grasped the brolly. These were beringed by a clutter of assorted flashy fat rubies, and an accumulation of tiny gold animals jangled merrily from the charm bracelet on her wrist.

'Probably a bookmaker's widow,' I mouthed, '. . . or she's just robbed a tomb.'

Joan, who, I am relieved to say, dislikes masses of jewellery, shrugged an indifferent response.

The queue suddenly moved a yard or so. In order to avoid bending for so short a time, I tried easing the cases forward with my foot. One case slid easily (mine!) but the other would not budge. I pushed even harder. Of course, when it did move there were no half-measures.

One second it was immovable, the next it had zipped across the floor into that powerful pair of ski-suited calves. The victim spun painfully around. I had certainly expected a hurt expression. Even so, I was not prepared for the battle-scarred countenance that faced me. Fifty years of boozing, fifteen kids, six husbands, countless family tragedies, or just one enormous, rip-snorting, storming good time, all could have caused that face. But *not* Joan's suitcase, most definitely not Joan's suitcase. No, not even if it had smashed her between the eyes every day for a year. Her 'Bugger you mate!' was, under the circumstances, not completely unexpected. My apology, however, dissolved rapidly into total amazement. If I had been fascinated by the rear of this woman, her front was astonishing.

There was now no doubt (absolutely none whatever!) that she was sixty. Yet the abdominal bulge under her tight-suited midriff made her appear seven months pregnant. In addition to this, the higher I looked the worse things became. Huge pendulous earrings were matched by huge pendulous breasts, on which dangled a crucifix almost half the size of the original. Yet all this paled into insignificance against her one really enormous blunder. This was her hair, or more accurately, her 'Fergi, Duchess of York' toupee. Apart from the obvious fact that it did not suit her a scrap, she looked – as Joan so quaintly put it – 'Like the Queen of Sheba in a wonky wig'. I could not take my eyes from it. The sheer angle of it held me spellbound.

'Oh, I'm sorry,' I finally blurted. 'I'm afraid the floor is quite slip – '

She suddenly cut me short by touching my arm. The change in her demeanour had been instant. 'Don't worry about it,' she assured me. 'Didn't really hurt anyway. It's just that I'm so wrought up about the flight.' She gave a rather helpless shrug. 'You see, I've never flown before and I'm a bundle of nerves. I'm not normally so rude.'

If the change in her had been instant, the change in me was as quick. One did not need to be the most perceptive person in the world to see the woman was absolutely petrified. I forgot about both the wig and the washing label. My suppressed hilarity conceded to immediate remorse.

'Oh, it's nothing to worry about,' I soothed. 'Joan here can't even look at a fairground without feeling sick – and she adores flying.'

The woman gave a weak laugh. 'I'm not sick, love . . . I'm terror struck!'

Further conversation was interrupted as two extra check-in desks were opened. Our queue quickly disintegrated for some minutes into a milling, case-colliding rabble. When order was finally restored, Joan and I found ourselves in a different line to both the woman and the quartet.

'Well, you can't say the SAGA passengers you've met so far have been boring, can you?' she asked.

'We've only really met one, so don't get carried away.'

'There were that nice foursome on the underground. They looked happy enough.'

'Yes, but we never actually spoke to them, did we? I mean for all we know they could be as mean as hell and not even speak English.'

'Well, they are English, they come from Leeds, because I saw their labels. In any case, you could tell by their faces what sort they were. It's a pity they're not in our party.'

'What do you mean "not in our party"? They had SAGA labels didn't they?' I asked.

'Yes, but they were on a different tour. In fact they were on the same tour as the lady with the wig. They are all off to Malta; she comes from Stepney, by the way.'

'What a little detective you are,' I marvelled. 'I'm quite disappointed that "Fergie" won't be on our tour now. Anyone of her age in a wig like that simply must be a character. I bet other than her fear of flying, she doesn't give a toss about anything.'

We had by this time reached the check-in. Not without difficulty, I slid both cases on to the scales and gave the receptionist our flight tickets. I had convinced myself that this was the moment when she would look up and say, 'Not a SAGA tour, sir, surely! You're much too young for that.'

I had decided I would not give her an audible answer to that question. Instead I would impart a smooth, relaxed and knowing wink. She scrawled across our documents, then clipped some papers together. Raising her head, she smiled.

Here it comes. I braced myself expectantly.

'Smoking or non-smoking, sir?'

My smooth, relaxed and knowing wink was countered by a puzzled expression and a further request for my smoking habits.

The treasures of the duty-free shop had only partially offset the blow I had suffered at the check-in, when Joan and I entered the lounge to pass the last hour before our flight. This is usually the time when I have long ceased trying to read, settling instead for just 'people-watching'. Apart from being cheaper, I fall asleep less often. The departure lounge of Heathrow is a perfect spot for this, sprinkled as it is with more poseurs per square yard than any other location in the land. In spite of my observations, it was Joan, peering over her *Daily Mail*, who first re-spotted Fergie.

If the lady had been distressed before, she was almost beside herself by then. She sat barely three yards from us in the next row of seats. A permanent cloud of smoke hung around her head, as she chain-smoked one cigarette after another, few of which she allowed to burn even halfway before lighting the next. In addition to her smoking, her trembles had also worsened and her wig was now practically on the side of her head. At the rate she was heading, she would be lucky(?) even to make the flight, now only minutes away.

'Go and chat to her,' requested Joan anxiously, 'else she'll have a breakdown before we even take off.'

'Why me?' I protested. 'You're a female, she'll feel more comfortable with you.'

'She'll feel nothing of the kind,' snorted Joan. 'She'd swim the oceans, that one, to even *talk* to a man. I recognize the type.' I knew she was right. I rose reluctantly to my feet. 'No – wait,' she whispered. 'Look, the two men from the Leeds quartet are going to speak to her. As they are in the same group, perhaps they are taking her under their wing.'

'Well, as I'm on my feet I may as well join them,' I sighed wearily. 'It's the least I can do after smashing her with your case.'

Although Fergie was in the next row, she was almost

within touching distance and we could hear every word clearly.

'Excuse me,' said the first happy puppy, in a tone I thought quite sharp, 'but can you read?'

The woman's jaw, which had been trembling like a tuning-fork, stiffened.

'Of . . . course . . . why?' she asked, with real effort.

'Because you're not allowed to smoke – that's why!' boomed the second equally happy puppy; '. . . which if you'd read the damn notice you'd have seen!'

The Stepney Queen could have received no greater therapy. She now had something tangible to fight. In fact, she had a double dose.

'Why, you pompous old prats!' she cried, leaping to her feet. 'I've been sitting here, scared out of me bleeding wits, and all the sympathy I get is you two daft bastards! Sod off, or I'll stick one on the pair of you!'

The men were visibly shaken, as indeed were their spouses. 'Eric! Hugo!' called one, 'Come back here, she's not worth it.'

The men beat a hasty retreat as Fergie, straightening both her wig and her shoulders, glowered after them.

'Now I come to think of it,' murmured Joan, obviously burying the 'happy puppy' theory for all time, 'they do look like an Eric and a Hugo.'

There must have been some twenty to thirty people scattered within comfortable earshot of that confrontation, yet not one of us acted as if anything unusual had taken place. The fact that a sexagenarian, wonky-wigged Amazon, surrounded by cigarette stubs in a non-smoking area, was hurling threats to a retreating, frightened, affluent-looking foursome, did not seem to register with anyone.

'British Airways announce the departure of their flight to Los Angeles . . .' Confirming this announcement by a glance at the information video, we all climbed to our feet. The difficulty some had in doing this seemed equated by the same number of SAGA labels.

'Oh well,' I muttered scornfully. 'I suppose it's wheelchairs to the fore. There's no chance of a late change of venue, I suppose?'

'Of course not,' she snorted. 'Where would you want to go anyway?'

'Malta, of course. I think that little fivesome are going to make for a rather interesting holiday. I bet she skewers at least one of 'em to her crucifix.'

Our plane was a 747, divided into three sections. Our seats were on the left side of the aircraft and in the front row of the centre section. Of the three seats on that side, the window seat was already occupied by a huddled little figure in a bulky brown overcoat. The head was totally covered by a thick woollen scarf. Without being too rude, I tried to discover the identity, or at least the sex, of the figure. After several abortive attempts, all I could decipher was that it was small, brown and female. I looked pointedly at Joan sitting on my right, then tilted my head towards the bundle of clothing on my left. She shrugged and leaned forward, but was obviously no more successful in her attempt to unravel the mystery.

As if in answer to our silent investigation, a young stewardess appeared. She explained that our travelling companion was an Ethiopian lady who was also bound for Los Angeles but spoke no English. She went on to request our indulgence in attending to the lady's needs throughout the flight.

'She feels the cold,' the girl rather needlessly pointed out.

It seemed uncharitable to say that I thought this attention was the function of stewardesses; we therefore assured her that the old (or young) lady would have our attention at all times.

I fixed the figure's seat belt and half a face appeared from beneath the folds of the scarf, wearing a small smile of gratitude. This at least gave me the chance to assess her age. She was younger than I had thought, no more than thirty or so. Drinks, food and duty-free were all eventually offered but, with a shy shake of the head, all were silently refused.

A couple of hours out from Heathrow, the cabin was darkened and the film began. This presented an immediate problem. We were too far forward and too much to the side to make much sense of the screen. In addition, the sound-track coming through our headsets appeared to have its origin on Mars. I gave up within minutes. Our Ethiopian guest was made of sterner stuff. Curled up in the corner of her seat she stared intently at the screen. The trouble was, it was the *wrong* screen. All her attention was devoted to the screen in the forward cabin, which by virtue of the angle of our seats, we could see more easily than our own. The problem was, we were watching *Hotel Du Lac*, but she was watching *Hannah and her Sisters*.

'She must have the wrong sound-track,' said Joan, pointing at the tuning switch on the seat arm.

When I checked, she certainly had the wrong sound. After studying the entertainment guide, I realized just how wrong. This Ethiopian lady who spoke no English was tuned into an audio-only channel. Its star attraction that day was Freddie Trueman giving an after-dinner speech on cricket! I pointed this out to Joan, who was not altogether surprised, saying that personally, she thought both Fred Trueman and cricket would make more sense to a vague Ethiopian than ever they did to her. Refusing to let this sacrilege wind me up, I turned out my reading light and was quickly asleep.

When I awoke, the film had long ended and most of the cabin was in darkness. Pinpoints of light denoted the most determined of readers. Sleeping bodies were either curled as close to each other as possible, or as far away as two seats would allow. I made my way to the lavatory at the rear of the plane. Dozily I stood poised over the stainless steel pan. It is at moments like this I can become very profound. What, I wondered, would my old grandfather have made of it all? In the space of little more than a generation things had changed so much. The old man's idea of a holiday was a crate of brown ale and a charabang ride to Southend. Yet here I was, his eldest grandson, 35,000 feet up, half asleep and urinating over the mid-Atlantic.

God, I felt proud.

About an hour out of Los Angeles, the stewardess handed each passenger an immigration card. These needed to be completed if we were to be allowed into the country. Now I am not good with forms. Never in my life have I correctly completed any form first time of asking. That night was no exception. I was finishing my third when my Ethiopian companion tapped me lightly on the shoulder. She wore a faint smile and nodded encouragingly as she handed me her card – her empty card. I was obviously expected to fill it in for her. This amused Joan no end.

'That's a laugh if you like,' she chortled. 'You of all people! Because you've filled in three she probably thinks you're an expert. Poor kid. She'd get through better with Fidel Castro.'

In the absence of Mr Castro, I gave it to the stewardess, who appeared about as clued-up as I was. She assured the lady in loud, slow English that she did not need to fill the thing in after all. The woman just smiled yet again and nodded.

A common thought is probably shared by all foreign visitors landing at USA airports. Namely, America does not want you there in the first place. The quickest I have ever passed through their immigration is an hour. Usually it is nearer two. We zig-zagged up and down the barriers until we reached the immigration control desk. We were there simply as tourists but by the time the desk was reached, I felt like a major in the KGB. A large, uniformed, butch-type woman bulged over her chair. She studied my passport photograph without a smile on her face. (Bad sign, this.) Glancing up to compare features, she demanded, 'Reason for visit?'

I faltered over each succeeding question. It was 'Er,' this and 'Um,' that, until at long last the reprieving stamp crashed down on the visa page.

A yard or so past the desk, I waited patiently whilst Joan's interrogation was completed.

'You two together?' asked Butch in a surprisingly sweet change of tone.

'Why, er, yes,' I bleated. 'Yes, of course.'

She smiled a broad admiring smile and nodded towards the SAGA label on Joan's hand luggage. 'Sure is wonderful, honey, how you old folk can get around nowadays. Sure is . . . sure is . . .' she echoed.

I wondered what the penalty would be for throttling a United States Immigration Official. It might just be worth it. It might just be . . . it might just be . . .

Sennapod Memories of Old London Bridge

The package-tour arrival at any foreign airport is a constant source of wonderment to me. I find the sheer logistics bewildering. To plonk down a plane-load of tourists in some strange land, for two long weeks, in a dozen or so different hotels, is mindblowing. But then, I couldn't organize a doze in a deckchair. Small wonder I am amazed when, within seconds of entering a foreign hotel, some smiling receptionist hands me a key in an envelope, with my name and room number already inscribed. If the airport is as busy as Los Angeles, I am even more impressed.

This journey was no exception. Emerging through immigration, we were instantly claimed by a petite, but not so young, female courier. She wore a conspicuous SAGA label across one inconspicuous breast, and the name tag 'Stella' across the other. We had ambled through in pairs, like claimants to the Ark. Each tired twosome was swiftly directed to a waiting coach – or as Americans will always say – bus. Ten minutes later, forty-one people paid only tired attention as Stella recited our names.

My first reaction was one of pleasant surprise. My ageist fears were obviously unfounded. At least a third of the party were of my own age or younger, and even many of the older ones *looked* younger. We were a fairly cosmopolitan bunch, with eighteen Britons, seventeen Americans and eight Canadians.

'That is forty-one replies out of forty-three names, folks,' said a puzzled Stella. 'Any ideas?'

'One will certainly be my husband Benjamin,' said a very smart sexagenarian from the rear of the bus. 'He's inclined to go walkabout if I'm not looking. Ah! There he is now.'

She pointed along the pavement to where a tall, smartly-blazered ex-military type strolled leisurely towards us. He was accompanied by another elderly man, very different in appearance. The second man was short, stocky of build and dragged his left leg behind him as if it were dead.

'And that one's my husband Reg,' said a dumpy west country lady near the front. 'I'm afraid he's recently had a stroke and not too good on his feet.'

Although we didn't know it at the time, this was a scene that was to be repeated many, many times during the next two weeks.

Benjamin was a classic visual advert for what most men would aspire to be at eighty. He was always immaculate and although he appeared to spend the whole fortnight in the same blazer, I never once saw it creased. A striped club tie was always impeccably knotted and his inch of white cuff was so precise as to be measured. A square, handsome, trimmed-moustached face was topped by a crown of thick silvery hair with never a thread out of place. Appearances, however, were deceptive. He was, as we were soon to discover, a wanderer. Whenever it was time to board the coach, he was rarely there. He would simply be sauntering around the area with a friendly, if faintly superior air, as if carrying out some partially secret survey for the Foreign Office.

His wife, Sylvia, was small, slim, and at sixty-seven years, still a surprisingly attractive woman. She appeared to have two main occupations in life. The first was losing Benjamin and the second one, finding him. I found her fascinating to talk to, but at least once each hour, she would ask in the most casual of tones – 'Haven't seen Benjamin I suppose? He has the money, you know.' I often wondered if Benjamin was quite as vague as he made out. Holding the cash as he did certainly assured Sylvia's continual interest in his whereabouts.

Reg, on the other hand, was a very different type. In theory he was a virtual cripple. The stroke had left him slow of speech and movement. In fact he spoke but rarely, and the leg he dragged so painfully around seemed to ensure total immobility. Yet he had the knack of appearing just about anywhere. He reminded me of a film I once saw called *Duel*, in which the driver of a powerful and fast sports car was unable to shake off a huge, lumbering juggernaut lorry. Whenever the driver looked in the mirror, whatever the speed and location, there was the lorry, right behind. Reg was like that. He was a tortoise to every hare. With his slow, stiff, scuffing movement, nothing seemed to be beyond him. He was encouraged in this by his strict wife, Molly, who rarely let him settle for long. She had cleverly ensured, by her discipline alone, his continual mobility.

'Well that's everyone, I guess,' sang out our courier as she turned to the driver. 'Okay Scott, let's hit the gas and get these good folks to their hotel.'

It took some forty-five minutes for the 'good folks' to reach their hotel. During that period Stella gave the customary welcome-aboard chat. She soon came over as an extremely professional woman with a sharp sense of humour. This was also a convenient time to begin to get acquainted with a few of our companions. The first we spoke to were Violet and Jean. They appeared friends of many years' standing but I was surprised to discover they had met for the first time on our flight from London. Voilet was a short, plump, energetic lady in her seventies, who still worked as a warden in an old people's sheltered housing unit in Manchester. Many of her charges were years younger than herself. She was an inveterate traveller and would toddle off cheerfully to anywhere that took her fancy. She was also an absolute charmer.

'Why California?' asked Joan.

'Don Ameche, luv!' replied Violet.

'Don Ameche?' I echoed, vaguely remembering the old-time smoothie of many a thirties or forties Hollywood musical. 'Must be a hundred if he's a day. Where on earth are you going to see him?'

'Ah'm not *seeing* him, luv,' she explained sweetly. 'Ah'm going to Grauman's Chinese theatre. Don Ameche's footprints are in the cement outside.'

'Good a reason as any,' approved Joan. 'How about Van Johnson? Are his prints in the cement?' This was a crafty dig at me. She had always been an admirer of Johnson but she also knew I could not stand him.

'Hopefully they buried him in the stuff,' I snapped, falling for the wind-up yet again. 'How about you, Jean?' I asked, changing the subject. 'Why're you here?'

Jean was a newly-retired secretary who looked a good ten years younger than her newly-retired age.

'Nothing as exciting as Van Johnson burial, I'm afraid.

Or even Don Ameche's feet, come to that. I came because I fancied it. That's all.'

We had by this time reached our hotel and, within seconds of alighting, had been allocated our rooms. Joan and I were soon established in a fourteenth-floor bedroom that faced south across the city. Although the humidity in Los Angeles was stifling, our room was freezing.

'The air-conditioning needs adjusting,' shivered Joan. 'D'you think you're up to it?'

This was, in truth, an understandable query. It must be said – I am *not* a mechanic. I am particularly not a *heating* mechanic. I once had an Austin A35 car for five and a half years and during that period was the record-breaking winter of 1963. But it was the summer of 1966 before I found out how the heater worked. I am equally efficient with air-conditioning.

After a ten-minute tinkering, I discovered this particular system gave the user three alternatives. Too hot. Too cold. Or a reasonable temperature with a deafening noise. Settling for the latter, we turned up the radio very loud and unpacked. The temperature certainly improved, but it did sound like *Music While You Work* in a munitions factory.

As I emerged from the shower, Joan drew my attention to the back of my body. It was covered in huge red weals. I groaned in self-pity. Every few days I suffer from an unknown allergy called urticaria, or hives. This results in large areas of the body from neck to knee being covered for several hours with these immensely irritating weals. They can vary in length from a pinprick to a couple of inches. I do have antihistamine which can prevent it and calamine which will ease it, but both items were tidily packed in my heavy brown brogues six thousand miles away on my bedroom floor.

'Let's go and look for a drugstore,' Joan suggested sympathetically.

I nodded. It was the only option open.

With collar up and sleeves down, I did my best to conceal the unsightly rash as we began our search. We were soon in luck. A large, old, untidy, rambling self-serve corner-store was just two streets away and appeared to sell just about everything. It was the sort of shop where the main problem was finding the item required. I doubt if even the proprietor knew what he stored. His shelf-fillers certainly didn't. We unsuccessfully searched the pharmacy and the nearest we could get to calamine was a tube of cream that Joan waved hopefully at me from across two gangways. On closer inspection, I dismissed it outright.

'Most definitely not!' I snapped. 'Nappy-rash ointment is OUT!!'

'But it's all there is,' she pointed out. 'Look, it's ten-thirty and even in Los Angeles that's pretty late to be buying bum ointment. It states on the tube . . .' she raised it to eye-level and read slowly . . . 'protects skin, relieves chafing, cuts, scrapes and sunburn. First choice of pediatricians for all diaper-rash cases. There, that should do you, don't you think?'

I knew she was right, of course. It *was* all we had. If it was to relieve the irritation, even a little, it would be an asset. Ungraciously I took the tube from her and took my place in the check-out queue.

She joined me a few moments later with a ninety-eight cents carton of orange juice. 'I thought we'd have this in our room before breakfast tomorrow,' she suggested.

There were some ten to fifteen people in the queue, all of them buying liquor, ranging from sour-mash to ouzo. As I shuffled nearer the cash-desk, I put down the carton and the tube and slid both items unthinkingly towards the cashier.

'Orange juice and diaper-rash cream, huh?' he muttered. 'Is that all?' I nodded. 'Well you folks sure have a hell of a good evening now,' he insisted, '. . . and don't you forget to come back tomorrow for another order, mind.'

Whether it was the embarrassment of the store or the effect of the ointment, I do not know, but within twenty minutes of my first application the rash began to fade and within an hour it was gone.

Other than feeling that the American Marine Corps were carrying out tank manoeuvres in the bedroom, we slept well. At least the temperature was good.

So it was reasonably refreshed that we emerged for breakfast next morning. We shared a table with Sidney. He was a bachelor, his build was slender – almost thin – and fading grey hair receded from a classically-featured face. He was aged about seventy-three and looked every year of it. Obviously 'chesty', he sounded a hundred.

Sometimes one needs a day or so to assess a fellow traveller, other times it can be done in minutes. This bloke we assessed in a little under fifteen seconds. Sidney St John Pears was my all-time winner for the world's eye-glazing championships. I realized that until I met Sid, I had never before really been bored. Oh yes, I *thought* I had – but really I hadn't. Sidney put that little matter right before he had buttered his toast. I had never imagined the relief a simple sentence like – 'Sorry, must leave, got a couple of things to do' – could give. As he left the room, having mentally screwed us to the floor for forty minutes, it was as if a dumper truck had been eased from my head.

Our reaction was a scene we were to see repeated many times throughout the next two weeks. In fact, in Las Vegas, one American lady (not from our tour) slid back her breakfast chair after fifteen minutes and with coffee in one hand and a croissant in the other, hysterically fled from the room saying, 'I must clean my shoes. I must clean my shoes.'

It was during this breakfast that we experienced a rare American phenomenon – a really dozy waitress. Probably because of the customary high standard of service in American restaurants, she tended to stand out. Certainly in London she would not have been considered as anything out of the ordinary, but in California she was a rarity. Breakfast was included in the tour cost and tickets were issued which the waitress collected when the meal was ordered. She collected them right enough, then promptly lost them, swearing we had never given them to her in the first place. She then disappeared completely for half an hour before re-emerging and asking for our tickets as if she had never seen us before. Finally taking our two orders, she succeeded in getting every item wrong, before completing her act by knocking a full glass of milk over my trousers.

'Well, honey,' she said, rubbing vigorously at my soaking genitals with a cotton towel, 'you sure drew the short straw this morning.'

At 8.30 a.m. the bus rolled up outside the hotel and forty-one of us were soon on board. Someone spotted Reg shuffling towards us two blocks away and a small search party soon found Benjamin.

Our first day was to be at Disneyland and Stella used the journey time to impart a few hints. 'To prevent congestion,' she said, 'you will find it better if you alight from the bus in two alternate sections. One day the driver's side is first, the next, the kerbside. This way you will get off the bus quicker and with fewer crushed toes.'

Now I thought this a pretty sensible and easily understood request. Yet for some reason Joan never seemed to get the hang of it. The fact that she has never been able to tell her left from her right did not help.

We were alighting in Arizona when she remained rigid in her seat. 'Just look at them,' she sighed despairingly. 'No matter what poor Stella says, they still get it wrong. It's *driver's* side today.' She gritted her teeth and remained unmoved, typifying her good old English stoicism when she *knows* she is in the right.

'It's *you*, you dozy cow!' I exploded. 'You've been here a week and you still haven't twigged that they drive on the other side of the road.'

Other hints passed out by the ever-thoughtful Stella were the totally different meanings of certain expressions in common usage on package-tours. She quoted Jean, who had forgotten her travelling clock and decided she needed an early call. Soon after our arrival, she had quite reasonably asked Stella if she could be 'knocked up' at six-thirty every morning. Because of Jean's age, Stella went to some pains to explain the difficulty of that request. 'Knocked up', in England, will mean little more than an early morning bang on the door. In America, it is the sole cause of pregnancy. As Stella explained, SAGA is a pretty accommodating company, but some things are just too late.

An hour or so later we entered the prairie-sized park

at Disneyland. Both Joan and I being pushovers for the place, we wandered around in permanent euphoria. Long before we left though, we wondered if Reg had been secretly signed by Disney. No matter where we went, from The Bear's Jamboree to Space Mountain, the old chap would appear moments later dragging his leg like a latter-day Long John Silver.

We returned to our hotel in the late afternoon, and as it was our first full day of the holiday, Stella had organized a get-together dinner. The actual meal was excellent, but such a dinner by itself has no climax. Soon the atmosphere began to dilute into chattering pairs. Suddenly one of the Canadians rose to his feet and pointed to the piano that stood in the corner of the room.

'Give me a dozen or so titles and I'll play you a medley you can sing along with,' he announced.

These titles were readily forthcoming, and with the panache of someone used to performing, he eased smoothly into a tuneful recital. The problem was, other than the actual titles, no one knew the words. Even people who had requested them knew little other than the opening verse. Sidney, who claimed to be an old theatrical, had promised a song but he retired to bed immediately after the apfelstrudel, complaining of nausea. The consensus of those around him suggested either divine intervention or poison.

During the course of the meal, I had noticed two vacant seats at an adjoining table. A few minutes after our lyric-less recital, an American couple made a belated, if unsteady, appearance. Herbert and Ursula were New Yorkers. They would have been New Yorkers even to people who had never set foot in America. I felt I had seen them hovering in the background of every James Cagney film.

Herbert, or as Ursula called him, 'Hoi-but', was a small dapper man with a sallow complexion and a deadpan face. Ursula, or as Herbert pronounced it, 'Oi-shula', was one of the plainest women I ever laid eyes on and a classic five-by-five. To add interest, they were both rather inebriated. They had, it appeared, been in the right hotel but the wrong reception.

A private function to introduce the interested parties to a sizable commercial project had been held in a small room on the floor directly above. They had innocently entered, but deliberately stayed. Whereas we had been supping a friendly little Californian white and a pleasant enough fruit-cup, they had been knocking back champagne and rather expensive claret. To say nothing of a little five-star brandy and the odd liqueur.

'Much bedder function al-ta-gedder up der,' pronounced Hoi-but thoughtfully. 'If you wanna go, just give dem my name.'

This lull in the evening's proceedings prompted Violet to keep both Joan and I entertained with stories of her previous travels. Having been mugged in Austria, she reported it to the police, who promptly slapped her into prison for twenty-four hours for wasting their time! Their theory being that no one in the land that spawned Hitler would ever dream of robbing a seventy-year-old widow. She therefore must have made up the whole story. It was two years later that her assailant, who was captured for a different offence, admitted the crime. This caused a constabulary panic that finally manifested itself in the form of a grand public apology and £200. This struck me as a pretty efficient way to keep crime figures low. Every time an offence is committed, slam up the victim! Must work like a charm.

Ironically enough, although the Austrians incarcerated her, the Bulgarians treated her like royalty. This was apparently caused by the 'occupation' she had shown on her passport. 'Warden', to the Bulgarians, was not some kindly soul who looks after a couple of dozen old folk, as much as some politically aware female who ran a high security prison. She was convinced that if she had been mugged in Bulgaria instead of Austria, the police would have shot ten hostages.

Joan asked her if she ever felt nervous traipsing around the world on her own.

'Bless you no, luv,' she chuckled, 'I'm more at risk back at the Home.'

'How's that?' asked a puzzled Joan.

'Well, it's some of them old boys, luv,' she explained. 'Randy old devils many of 'em. When I'm doing my daily checks, I sometimes knock on their doors and call through the letter box. "Are you alright, Mr Jones?" "I'd be a whole lot better if you came in, darlin'," they'll answer. You can't take your eyes off some of them old blokes for a minute, you can't.'

'So how old are they?'

'Eighty, many of them.'

'Eighty!' echoed Joan, a note of marvel creeping into her voice. 'Well, that *is* certainly something to look forward to!'

The following day was the highlight for me. As Catholics yearn for St Peter's, Muslims for Mecca and Jews for Jerusalem, so I have always hankered for Hollywood. Well, not only were we *in* Hollywood, but we were going to spend a whole afternoon in Universal Studios! I could now die happy.

Our tour of the studios was preceded by a visit to Grauman's Chinese theatre. Voilet stared down at Don Ameche's footprints in such a state of reverence, that any one of her over-sexed octogenarians could have spent a blissful twenty minutes behind her, without getting his face slapped.

That afternoon was a dream come true. Many of the sets were almost home to those of us who served their apprenticeships in the local bug-hole picture-places. There was the same bank (different names of course) we had seen robbed so many times. The *Psycho* hotel, the Andy Hardy picket-fenced house, King Kong (who roared loudly in my right ear), the western bridge (which disintegrated as we crossed), earthquakes, flashfloods, parting seas, the Great White Shark that leaped at us from out of still waters and of course, the stuntmen. Always the stuntmen. They spun from roof-tops and towers, some drunk, some sober, some shot, some punched. They fell out of windows and crushed through staircases.

'Have you ever noticed,' asked a perceptive but know-all voice from nearby, 'that in films, no one ever gets killed in a basement?'

'Good t'ing too,' snapped Hoi-but angrily. 'Who'd wanna see anyone killed in a basement? T'ain't no fun!'

As I watched yet another villain clutch at his bullet-ridden chest, spin crazily around and disappear into two somersaults from a dance-hall roof, I realized the wisdom of Hoi-but's words. There was unquestionably no fun in getting killed in a basement.

'In a little over an hour, we shall be in San Diego,'

announced Stella, 'and for my money, it's the loveliest city in the whole USA.'

This announcement had aroused me from a guilty doze, just in time to hear another comment, this time from the ever-attentive Violet. 'That town we just passed used to be an Ink Spots record.'

I almost ricked my neck looking back, but the name 'Capistrano' rang no bell.

'Never heard of it,' I pronounced.

'Never heard of it,' she mimicked. 'You mean to say you've never heard of *When The Swallows Come Back To Capistrano*?' She shook her head sadly. 'One of their very best.'

'It was shit,' sniffed Hoi-but, who had obviously woken from an even deeper sleep than I had.

Whatever the qualities of the song, it did succeed in focusing attention on the fact that there is barely a town, river or city-dump in south-west America that has not had a film, play or song written about it. This title spotting gradually became quite a competition amongst the British with some very obscure titles indeed being claimed.

San Diego was all we had been promised and after lunch we began a tour of the city with Henry, a local bus-driving guide. Henry was probably more of an entertainer than a guide, and for a sizable part of the time he kept us regaled with horror stories of his ex-wife and mother-in-law. ('My wife has the cat but she allows me visitation rights.') Having stopped in front of numerous impressive public and private buildings, we rolled to a needlessly noisy halt, smack across the driveway of a large, but otherwise unimpressive house.

'Nothing special about this place,' he agreed. 'Except to say the owner was once rude to me, so I stop here for four minutes on every tour. It makes him as mad as hell!' Checking his timer as meticulously as any commando, he snapped it off sharp at exactly four minutes and drove on. 'You may notice,' continued Henry, 'that certain parts of town are designated as "No Bus Areas". This is because of opposition from local residents. Not too much notice should be paid to this however, because at night certain bus drivers go out and change them around – the *signs* that is – not the residents.'

'He'd be a knock-out in Austria,' murmured Violet admiringly. 'If I got twenty-four hours for being mugged, he'd get life for changing road signs.'

For our two-day stay in San Diego, we were based in a Mission Bay motel. On the afternoon of our second day, we visited Sea World, which is a vast Oceanarium (*their* word, not mine!) some two miles distant. Some twenty of us were dropped off by bus and soon went our own ways.

Some five hours later, the pair of us emerged and decided on a leisurely walk back to our motel. We strolled to the corner of the car park nearest to our destination. There was no exit. To leave the car park, one went either back into Sea World or out on to the freeway. There was no other route. Neither were there directions or a footway. Quite simply, an entertainment centre that catered for thousands did not cater for any of them who might be on foot! On the forty-minute stroll back to our motel, the drivers of three separate vehicles all kindly stopped to enquire as to our welfare. Simply because we were walking.

Our return coincided with that of Jean, who had been shopping downtown. She had returned via the city bus service and did not look happy.

'I'm furious over that damn bus,' she seethed. 'I've just travelled from the city centre and he only charged me forty cents.'

'So?' we both said in unison.

'So?' she echoed. 'D'you know what he said to me?' Without waiting for a reply she thundered on. 'He said "Senior citizens forty cents". That's what he said!'

I sighed. 'Look, I hate to say this again, Jean – but *So?*'

'Well, I *know* I am over sixty but I really do resent it when other people *assume* it!'

'So you would have been happier paying two dollars instead of forty cents?'

'Of course.'

'I can understand how she felt,' Joan said to me later. 'She really doesn't look anywhere near sixty. No wonder she was annoyed. I would have been.'

'Oh, I see!' I cut in triumphantly. 'Yet when I wouldn't put a SAGA label on my baggage, I was a "vain old sod".'

'Well, it's different for ladies,' she sniffed.

Having made a token trip to Mexico to sample the dubious delights of Tijuana (as far as I could see, this consisted of dentists and leather belt sellers), our route then took us north-east towards the Grand Canyon. To do this, we needed an overnight stop. This we made at a hotel on the shore of Lake Havasu. It was particularly poignant for me to walk the bank of this lake, because there, on the edge of the Arizona desert, was London Bridge. *My* London Bridge. The London Bridge where I spent half a childhood. The London Bridge that I crossed every day as I cycled to my first job. It now leads nowhere. It just sits there – I swear it is getting fat – serving no other purpose than that of a monument. A bridge put out to grass. Who ever heard of such a thing?

I just stood staring for a while. I could not believe how sad I felt. I wondered what Rosie Pilbeam and Charlie Martin from my childhood would have said. They never even survived the first two months of the blitz, yet the bridge survived the whole damn war. Fancy surviving all those bullets, bombs and mines just to be kidnapped and dumped down on the edge of a desert six thousand miles from home. Still, who knows, perhaps the old bridge enjoys the eternal sunshine. If it does, then who can begrudge it? Least of all me.

I was not the only one to be affected by sentiment and nostalgia. Sidney too had known the bridge. Not as a child, though; it was simply that he had worked nearby in the city for a time in the 1920s.

Sidney was one of those people completely preoccupied with the precise regularity of their bowels. He always did his best to ensure that others were equally fascinated.

'Crossed this bridge every Friday without fail,' he informed Scott, our puzzled driver. 'Most important mission it was too . . . most important,' he emphasized. 'Always came here to a chemist's to buy the old sennapods. Mum swore by them. Regular as clockwork we were, the whole household. We used to have a rota system outside our garden lavatory every Saturday morning. You can't beat a good clear-out, I say.'

Other than the bridge, the only thing to impress in Havasu was a cockroach that took over our bathroom. Although it was slightly smaller than a Rottweiler, it had more legs. Fifty of them could have taken over the world.

It was this hotel that gave us such a problem with its electric light fittings. I don't think they had been installed for any functional purpose, more to impress. For example, if a guest actually managed to turn off the bedside lamp at night, he would doubtless sleep well, with a sense of achievement and with the air of a task well done. Yet we discovered next day there were other problems besides sleeping at nights, such as waking in the mornings.

Because of the absence of her clock, and her lack of enthusiasm for pregnancy, Jean had requested an early call. At 6.30 a.m. the bell rang, but the room being dark, she was unable to find the receiver.

Still the bell rang.

Reaching for the bedside lamp, she found everything except the switch to turn it on.

Still the bell rang.

The only alternative seemed to be the switch on the wall by the door. But she got lost.

Still the bell rang.

Back-tracking to the telephone again, she tripped over furniture and crashed to the floor.

Still the bell rang.

Finally finding the lead, she followed it hand-over-hand until she reached the mouthpiece. She lifted it from its housing – the bell stopped ringing. Bruised, bewildered, close to tears and breathless, she lay on the floor in the dark amidst a jumble of overturned furniture.

'Hullo, Hullo,' she panted.

'Six-thirty mam,' trilled a voice. 'You have a nice day now.'

Jean had recounted this disaster to us soon after boarding our bus for the Grand Canyon. I remember being surprised how attentive Sidney seemed. It just was not like him. He hardly ever listened to anyone – only himself. Yet he sat gazing straight at her and nodding approval at her every word. His cover was blown at the end of her tale however, when he sat straight up, looked all around and said, 'Yes, but what I could never understand about that place was how the lights worked.'

We arrived at our hotel in mid-afternoon. It was laid out in the shape of a log cabin compound, just two storeys high and very comfortable. The Canyon was now only a ten-minute drive away. Dumping our cases, we were all soon back on the bus and, within minutes, surely one of the most breathtaking sights in the world was laid out before us. Because of a warning of heavy turbulence, in addition to the usual heart and respiratory dangers, few of our party had booked for a Canyon flight. These trips are carried out by small aircraft (eight to ten very cramped seats) that fly low over the stunning landscape. Having purchased tickets, our small group made its way across the narrow runway to where our plane had recently landed.

With just a little difficulty, we climbed into our seats and, just as I thought we were to take off, the pilot called, 'We're still one short. Anyone have a friend missing?'

I glanced back to the office. Sure enough, right on cue, there was Reg dragging his leg behind him. The pilot shook his head in silent disbelief as a uniformed helper eased the old chap up and through the small door and into the tiny seat.

Throughout the flight Reg remained totally unmoved. The 'Ooohs!' and 'Ahhhs!' that exploded from the rest of us were not for him. He just stared, mainly at the rear of the pilot's head, or alternatively, through the side window. On landing, it took us longer to get him to his feet than it did to explore the Canyon.

Before dinner that evening, one more bus trip was

scheduled. This was to take place at seven o'clock and was to be back from whence we had come – the Canyon. The reason was twofold. There was a crystal-clear sky and it was sunset. Even more good luck had ensured an early rise to the moon. The rocks appeared illuminated as vast belts of fiery colours swept steadily across the whole panorama. Then, as blackness fell, the palest silvery glow penetrated all but the deepest parts of the Canyon. Although the temperature fell rapidly and we suddenly found ourselves shivering, it was a memorable sight.

It had been an enjoyable day and we said as much to our waiter's polite enquiries as he led us to our table at the hotel dinner. Jean and Violet joined us in a foursome.

'Well, hi once more, folks,' greeted our waiter as we sat down. 'I'm yours for the evening and my name is Bruce. Anything I can do for you folks, anything at all mind, you just let me know. I'll be back for your orders soon.'

He had barely left when another waiter approached our table. He was a large young man in his early twenties and very similar to his predecessor, except he wore strong, pebble-lensed spectacles.

'Hi folks!' he greeted us, equally cheerfully. 'I'm Joseph, Bruce's assistant. Now if there's anything I can do for you . . . well I guess you know the rest.'

'A waiter and an *assistant* waiter?' queried Violet, expressing all our thoughts. 'I've never heard of that before. That's one more than I had in the whole of Bulgaria!'

The system worked pretty well, that is until pudding time, when Jean discovered she was a spoon missing. She then called several times to the passing Bruce but he did not seem to hear. Meanwhile, Joseph, who was hovering over a distant table, did glance our way from time to time, yet still failed to respond to our waves.

'I've cracked this!' said Joan suddenly. 'Assistant-to-Bruce indeed! That's just a ploy.'

'What d'you mean?' I asked.

'Well, we've called Bruce and he don't hear. We've waved to Joseph but he don't see. I think one is deaf and the other's blind!'

'Well, we'll hide the tip, luv,' said the perceptive Violet, 'and see who finds it. That should tell us.'

But we were never to discover the secret of Joseph and Bruce, primarily because Joan spotted Sidney making a royalty-like tour of each table, sharing a few words here and a whole speech there. 'Look out! Sidney!' came the dreaded cry.

Four cups of coffee were drained in unison and four chairs were slid back just as quickly. So we never did see who was collecting the tip. For all I knew it could have been Sidney; and if that meant not hearing about his bloody bowels again, I would have considered it money well spent.

On leaving for Las Vegas next morning, our route was to take us once more to the Canyon. I was delighted at this because it seemed sacrilegious to spend just one day in such a beautiful spot. This time we were introduced to a local guide who took us for a short walk along the Canyon escarpment. He certainly knew his job but insincerity oozed from him.

'Hi folks!' he greeted us. 'My name is Wilbur, friends.'

'Wilbur Friends?' queried a puzzled Violet. 'That's a funny name.'

The newcomer was a large, stocky man with a big red

face and an even bigger stetson hat, which he had great difficulty retaining on his head in the breeze. As he had begun to speak, shafts of sunlight had broken through the clouds that had gathered overnight.

He nodded down in the Canyon to where a particularly sharp shaft had begun to play on a great red boulder. 'Glory be!' he exclaimed, 'it looks like the Old Master Painter is shining His spotlight down on the rocks just for you good folks.' He gave a little forced chuckle. 'Well, Ah for one don't blame Him. You sure are one wonderful group.'

'Yuk! Yuk!' whispered Joan.

'It's a great shame you folks do not have a longer time here. Ah would dearly love to lead you down on a mule to that great Colorado River down there.'

'I don't t'ink der mules would like ter carry me very much,' observed the plump Oi-shula.

'Mam,' said Wilbur reverently, 'those mules would *love* to carry you! They accept all you good folks who come all this way to see us, as a pure labour of love. Those creatures are never happier than when you good folks are sitting on their backs.'

'I think I'm going to be sick,' said Joan.

I had to agree. Yet within minutes he did something that completely won me over. We had walked on a little and arrived at a place called The Hermit's Rest.

'See that huge bell?' called Wilbur. 'For some people that can be very lucky. If you've had a run of bad luck, this could be where it all changes.' He pointed to where a sturdy black bell hung down from a short beam that bridged two wide posts. It was hanging some seven or eight feet above the ground. 'Anyone had a run of bad luck lately?'

A sad-looking American lady came shyly forward. Even just looking at her face I think we all knew that life had not been kind to her.

'You been unlucky, mam?'

She nodded, almost imperceptibly.

'Okay mam. Now you stand quite still here with your back to the bell.' He positioned her some five yards from the beam. 'Now you take this pebble in your left hand and throw it hard over your shoulder. If you can ring that bell your luck will change – ready?'

'He shouldn't do this!' I hissed, 'that woman's close to tears.'

We knew it was supposed to be a joke but there was something about the woman that bothered us. He handed her a small round stone. Biting her bottom lip, she weighed it up and down rapidly a few times and then threw it sharply in an arc over her left shoulder. It missed the bell by half of a cricket pitch. She wasn't even in the right direction. In following the flight of *her* stone, I almost missed the flight of *his*. It struck the bell smack amidships and a fine healthy DONG! reverberated out across the Canyon. His throwing hand was thrust comfortably back in his pocket for almost a full second before the woman turned, her face transformed.

'Ah tell you this, mam,' he assured her. 'In all mah years here, Ah've never known such a decisive ring. Ah would guess you are soon due to be one lucky lady.'

'But – ' began Sidney, edging forward.

Yet he had hardly moved before his arm was roughly seized by Hoi-but, who then turned him and eased him none too gently away from the group.

'You've got it wrong, Sid,' he whispered. 'She made the best damn t'row you'll ever see. Geddit?'

Sid got it.

It was on the way back to the bus that the alert was first raised for Reg and Benjamin. Sylvia realized she had not seen either of them since our arrival on the escarpment.

'Not bad judges, missing Wilbur,' murmured Violet enviously. 'Wish I'd thought of it meself.'

'There they are!' called a voice. 'Going down that narrow path into the Canyon.'

We each craned forward. Sure enough, there they were, some three hundred yards down into the Canyon and picking their way between stones and tree roots. They were so unconcerned they could have been on Brighton pier – except that the unfenced drop, eighteen inches from their shoulders, was probably a mile deep.

'Don't let him go any further,' sighed Sylvia wearily. 'He's got *all* my traveller's cheques.'

The journey from the Canyon to our next stop took us via the Hoover Dam, across the Nevada desert and on to Las Vegas. The ride was quite successful. We managed to keep possession of both Reg and Benjamin in the desert and no one pushed Sidney off the dam. As Stella commented, 'Quite a result.'

I think Las Vegas is one of the very few places I have ever seen that turns out to be *exactly* what I imagined. Yet even I was surprised by the first sign that greeted us. It was erected in front of a small white wooden chapel. It read: WEDDINGS AND GRAND CANYON FLIGHTS ARRANGED.

I couldn't help the feeling that you could not have one without the other and that no Vegas wedding was consummated without a five-minute spin up the Canyon.

*

Give or take a little, the hotels on our trip had been good; some bordered on excellent. Our first impression of the Mexicali in Las Vegas was that it was well up to this standard. Our bus had barely stopped before our room-keys were placed in our laps in thick, embossed, name-stamped envelopes, with two days' supply of restaurant tickets. Our cases were then spirited upstairs and, with equal efficiency, we were led to our rooms. Then . . . the wheel began to come off.

Firstly, there were the double bookings. At least a third of our party experienced them. Secondly, and this had little to do with the hotel, everything else that could go wrong, did. This was probably best typified by Sylvia and Benjamin. Each couple had been provided with two keys. As Sylvia began to unpack and bath, Benjamin wandered off. Ninety minutes later, although Sylvia had by then changed and bathed, Benjamin had still not reappeared. Locking the door, she went to look for him. She found him within minutes but on her return, her key broke in the lock. A locksmith was sent for and attended rather quickly. But whilst he was working on the lock, Benjamin wandered off again. The task was soon completed, so Sylvia, with her new key for the new lock, searched once again for Benjamin. Whilst she searched, he returned. With, of course, his old key, which he promptly broke in the *new* lock.

Meanwhile, Hoi-but and Oi-shula had sought out Stella, our courier.

'I have a complaint to make,' he announced. 'Dere are two half-naked broads in my room . . . and my wife won't let me sleep with eidder of dem.'

Violet also found her room occupied. Two bearded men and two punk-rock ladies had been drinking bourbon and smoking a 'substance'. When Violet's key turned in the door, they thought it was a mature member of the FBI. (Shades of Bulgaria?) One of the girls slammed herself in the bathroom and flushed the lavatory for twenty minutes.

Not to be outdone in the general insanity of our arrival, Sidney ran into the hotel's tennis professional. With his shorts, sweat-shirt, two rackets and sack of tennis balls, he could barely have been mistaken for anything else. Sidney put that right by asking him if he taught golf.

'No!' said the man icily, waving both rackets. 'Tennis, man. Tennis!'

'I see!' exclaimed Sidney with unaccustomed interest, '. . . and where are you in the world?'

'Pardon?' asked the bemused coach.

'In the *world*,' repeated Sidney. 'You know . . . in the world? Where would you say you are?'

'You mean *rankings*?'

'Ah yes, that's it!' agreed the probing Sid. '*Rankings!* Where are you in the *rankings*?'

'Well, in the *world* I'm shit,' he replied. 'But I'm number one at the Mexicali.'

This conversation almost reduced the listening Jean to wet knickers, which caused her no little worry. The reason for her alarm was that she had washed three pairs immediately on arrival. She wrung them all out in a towel but forgot to hang them up. Because of the confusion over double bookings, the maid played it safe and dashed quickly around and changed all the towels. Jean therefore found herself with three new towels but minus three pairs of drawers.

By and large, Joan and I had been particularly lucky with our room. Of course we could not work the light switches and the air-conditioning froze us to the marrow but what the hell – wasn't Vegas a gambling town?

It was that assumption that caused the pair of us to go for a walk along 'The Strip'. Within minutes we experienced the greatest gamble in the whole city – crossing the road on foot. When pedestrians appear in front of the average Las Vegan motorist, it is like a reaction test on a sniper's course. He feels he has three-fifths of a second to decide if he should kill, or simply maim you a little. Usually he prefers to kill.

He will then broadcast the progress of his attempt over his CB radio. 'Two middle-aged limeys, north along The Strip. Angels-one-five, attacking in formation . . . GERONIMO!!!'

The healthy pedestrian will finally reach Caesar's Palace. This is a huge hotel about half the size of Rome. Arrival will be by pure natural selection as only the fittest would have survived the fifty-minute walk. A loud metallic voice booms at you, welcoming 'Caesar's Special Guest'. It will then suggest an astounding amount of ways to separate you from your money. If the real Caesar spoke with anything like the sincerity of his Las Vegas counterpart, I am not surprised his best friend did him in. I should imagine all his other friends were only furious that they too could not have buried their daggers, preferably in his throat.

In order to fortify ourselves for the journey back, we decided to buy an ice-cream. Where but in America would one buy a traditional Italian soft ice-cream in a petrol station? The problem was it was self-serve. I gave sixty cents to a cashier, who gave me a large cone. I held it beneath a tube and pulled a lever. I had just assumed there would be a cut-out switch. There wasn't. Ice-cream cascaded out like a dam-burst. Within seconds, I was trying to balance thirteen inches of ice-cream on a five-inch cone. If the outgoing journey was difficult, the return trip, clutching and balancing a mountain of runny ice-cream, was a nightmare. Motorists came from the whole state of Nevada to try their luck on us.

Undoubtedly the best value in Vegas, usually, are the hotel meals and shows. These are cheaply priced and mainly of good quality. Of course, this is primarily to place the customer within reach of the gaming machines and tables.

That night, half of our group had booked in for our hotel's show – 'Minsky's Burlesque'. This was an eighty-minute show where the jokes were like hearing from an old school friend. The finale, on the other hand, was nothing *whatever* to do with school. It featured an acrobatic and stunningly deformed young lady, who bent forward over the front row and performed such a feat of mindblowing mammary gyrations that, sitting in the second row, I felt nearer to her nipples than she was. I was interested to see that at the end of her act, the ladies of the SAGA group applauded as much as their menfolk. Although for some reason that I never did discover, Sidney thought she was a skater!

Later in the bar, Scott, our bus-driver, asked what we thought of the show. 'Was it tasteful?' he asked, with just a hint of concern.

'Sure was,' Hoi-but assured him. 'I was in der thoid row and I could taste it beautifully.'

To head west from Las Vegas entails a long drive across the Mojave desert. Our bus, though air-conditioned, had begun to radiate a persistent smell of something dead.

Sidney appeared to be still moving, so that just left the small toilet at the rear of the vehicle. This turned out to be faultless, so a small sniffing party began to inspect each seat.

The smell was finally traced to the bag of a sweet but highly embarrassed, shy Scots lady, who had hardly spoken a word on the tour. Three days before, she had ordered a steak dinner, but from the outset it proved too much for her. She had barely touched the meat, and felt that the chef would be upset if he saw the amount left uneaten. She therefore wrapped it in a serviette and slipped it into a small holdall. Unfortunately, she had then forgotten it, and after three days in constantly changing temperatures it was making its presence known.

We held our breath as Scott eased the bus into the side of the road. A grimacing Stella, holding the fomenting steak like a suspect grenade, hurled it far into the desert.

'I just hope that spot is not an old Indian burial ground,' she said anxiously, 'because that steak is such heap bad medicine, they'll haunt me for the rest of my life.'

We were heading for Fresno, which was to be our last stop before San Francisco. We broke for lunch at a town called Bakersfield. This would have been a completely unmemorable stop, except for that same lunch.

Scott cheated a little and parked our bus in a McDonald's restaurant, even though few of us intended to lunch there. Joan and I strolled up the main street and were returning when we saw a full-scale wedding-party. It consisted of several huge limousines, a glamorous bride, morning-suited groom and twenty-five to thirty splendidly attired guests. The whole show looked a typical affluent middle-class nuptial, the sort that could be seen on most Saturdays in any shire town in Britain. The difference was that this reception was actually held *in* McDonald's! The only preference shown to this party was that their tables were reserved. But they still had to queue for their hamburgers – even the bride and groom!

'Before you British say a word,' cut in Stella, as we reboarded our bus. 'No, I have never *ever* seen a wedding in McDonald's before – and no, it is *not* a quaint old American custom.'

'I think the whole thing's a blow to your colonial pride,' teased Jean.

'Probably wot yer git fer not takin' der Grand Canyon flight on yer weddin' I s'pose,' said the helpful Hoi-but.

Even its town council would probably not rate Fresno very high on any tourist itinerary but it rates unbeatable on my list of honesty. One regularly hears much of city crime in the USA and when we arrived, late that afternoon, a large open-air market was being held in the centre of town. Around 10 p.m., during an after-dinner stroll, we passed the market again. It was still full of goods: coats, dresses, fridges, TVs, recorders etc., but all the stall-holders had long gone home. The only security for tens of thousands of dollars' worth of readily disposable goodies was a band of white tape and a newspaper-reading security guard, who seemed more than happy to pass half an hour in conversation with us.

Equally impressive, albeit for a different reason, were the hotel taps in Fresno; or as Americans persist in calling them, 'faucets'.

Like their confounded light switches, every American bathroom has a different tap system. It can be the devil's own job to fill a bath or a washbasin and as for a *shower*, well, they run three-day courses. (Though no British tourist has ever succeeded in passing.)

To obtain water, some taps turn. Some taps lift. Some taps press. Some taps push and some taps actually wiggle. (Or as our German-American lady from Philadelphia said – much to Sidney's confusion – 'Zum tips voggle.')

When these showers work, boy how they work! A torrent force of volcano-quenching water smashes down on, or against you. One does not so much stand *under*, as lean *against*, the spray. This can cause all sorts of problems.

On the way to dinner, Violet looked quite harassed. 'I've lost me glasses,' she muttered.

'Well you had them when we checked in,' Joan pointed out.

'I know, luv,' she agreed. 'But I took them off when I went for a shower, but then I couldn't work the thing. I then put them back on to fix it but the water came on with such a force that it swept them off me face and I couldn't find them anywhere. So I had a bath instead.' She gave a long sigh. 'I said to meself, Oh bloody hell, Violet, it's time you stayed at home, you pudden'.'

Next day, and still not risking a shower, we left for the last lap of our tour – to San Francisco. For the final two and a half days our holiday was to take on an entirely different aspect. The tour as such, was over. We were now on our own. It is what is referred to in holiday-brochure English as 'free time'. This is, of course, complete nonsense. Whatever it is, it isn't 'free'. No package-tour operator will spirit you to the end of your street – never mind California – for *free*. No, the free time is not for you, it's for the company. They no longer have to drive you or feed you. On the other hand, you can sleep longer in the mornings. Or the afternoons too for that matter. To be fair, the holiday loses nothing by this. In fact, in San Francisco, it is probably the best policy to adopt.

Both Joan and I loved the town. We did all the usual touristy things, such as the Golden Gate Bridge and Alcatraz prison, and at the slightest opportunity we would be on a trolley-car down to Fisherman's Wharf. I would stare open-mouthed at each wide junction, convinced I had seen at least two films that had been shot there, ranging from Laurel and Hardy to *Bullitt*. At first it felt strange not to chuckle over some commonsense homily from Violet, or a sharper style of comment from Hoi-but. Yet in two and a half days, in a city of three-quarters of a million people and thirty thousand hotel bedrooms, we still managed to run into the limping Reg no fewer than three times, once in the exercise yard at Alcatraz!

We did have one close call; this was at breakfast where we actually sat at a table next to Sidney. He spent most of the time talking to a partially deaf American matron, who for some reason thought he was discussing oil. He was in fact talking about hops. For thirty-five minutes the pair of them had two totally different conversations, without a clue as to what the other was saying. I did enjoy that.

'I think you're tempting fate by laughing,' said Joan, as we strolled out after breakfast. 'I bet you haven't thought about the return journey.'

'What about it?'

'Well, your Ethiopian dependant was on a one-way flight. Leastways, we haven't seen her since we landed.'

'So?'

'So who else do you know who is on their own and due back on our plane?'

'No one – wait a minute! You don't mean Sidney, surely?'

'Of course I mean *Sidney*. It's the obvious place to put him. Window seats go in threes. So if we get a window seat there will be one odd space alongside us. So it's a fair bet that we'll have him. I just thought you ought to mentally prepare yourself, that's all.'

'To mentally prepare myself for Sidney, I will need to walk on the wings. No, there has to be a better way than that.'

'Name it.'

'Okay,' I snapped decisively. 'Here it is. When the bus arrives to take us to the airport, we'll watch carefully where Sidney is sitting. Then we'll sit as far away as possible, so if he is near the door, we'll go to the back of the bus. That way we will arrive at the check-in several entries after him.'

Now this was an excellent idea – in theory. In practice, Sidney certainly sat near the door. In practice, we did manage to sit at the rear of the bus. In practice, Sidney was certainly on his feet first. In practice, every snivelling, cowardly, return-traveller to London remained seated en masse.

'I don't know why you're all concerning yourselves so much,' stage-whispered Stella. 'He's not returning to London anyway. He's going on for two weeks to visit a niece in Chicago.'

There was an immediate rumbling, like a theatre audience trying to beat the national anthem. Within seconds we were all out on the pavement saying goodbye to the Americans and Canadians and then most of all, Stella. Without a doubt, she had been the most professional guide I had ever travelled with.

Sidney approached each of us in turn to make his farewell. I suddenly felt quite guilty about my attitude towards him. Fortunately, he had either developed a thick skin over the years, or he genuinely did not notice. I suspected the latter. The glassy stare that came over folks as he updated his bowel movements he obviously confused with idolatry.

It seemed no time before our flight was called, and with their customary immaculate timing, Benjamin and Reg had wandered off three minutes previously. However, our fifth search party of the tour soon found them (where else but in the duty-free) and twenty minutes later we were all aboard.

'I'll tell you this,' announced Joan decisively. 'In spite of all your daft misgivings, I would happily come on a SAGA tour again. Wouldn't you?'

'Ah! I'm pleased you reminded me,' I replied, gratefully. 'I must take those SAGA labels off our hand-luggage now, and off our suitcases as soon as we reclaim them.'

She raised her eye-brows wearily; '. . . And if your next topic is going to be *your* constipation, just stay where you are and *I* will walk on the wings!'

A Long Walk in the Madeiran Bush

I hate Ken Dodd. I have for more than twenty years. It is nothing really personal, just a sort of chemical reaction I suppose. A harmless petty prejudice of the sort that most people experience from time to time. I certainly never thought it would amount to anything more than that. I mean, I never expected to have a sudden rush of blood to the head and blow up the Diddy-Men, for example. No, I simply thought I would always be able to quell my abhorrence by leaping quickly to the off-button and pressing it ferociously hard, whenever he appeared on TV.

I considered my dislike to be purely one-sided. After all, Mr Dodd would be totally unaware of my existence, never mind my paranoia. He would sail obliviously on his sweet way, whilst I slowly enjoyed, perhaps even revelled in, my dislike of those protruding teeth, storm-shocked hair and inane chat. Why then, I still wonder, could this uncharacteristic neurosis on my part threaten my potential demise on a Madeiran mountainside? Yet it certainly did.

It began one bright May Tuesday morning in Funchal (capital of Madeira). Most Madeiran mornings are bright. This is to give the tourist enough sunshine time for a leisurely breakfast and an amiable discussion of the day's programme, before the clouds build up and the rain comes down. This particular morning, I was awakened at 7.30 a.m. by the sounds of large lorries and loud voices.

On parting the curtains, I could see easily into the beautiful park next-door. Even at that early hour, it was obvious that something big was about to break. For not only were 'sets' being built, but TV generators, cables and cameras were being manoeuvred into place.

'Is the president coming?' we wondered.

The pleasantly plump, smiling waitress at breakfast quickly resolved the mystery.

'No! Not the president!' she derided. 'Someone far, far more important than any president.'

The town was to be graced it seemed, for the next four days, by a Portuguese TV personality with an unpronounceable name. There was to be a sort of Madeiran 'It's a Knockout' tournament but the coverage was not to be confined to that subtle game alone. There were to be beauty competitions, parades, floats and processions. Having gone to the expense of sending a TV crew to the island, the company was determined to obtain the most for its money. The town, therefore, was expected to enjoy its visiting 'royalty' to the full. Could be interesting, I thought, as I sat on the hotel sunroof and watched the sets take shape and the crowd assemble.

Soon it was rehearsal time. The director murmured instructions to a lackey, who in turn screamed them at the scores of auditioning competitors and even at the crowd itself. Then a roar arose from the waiting throng, as the personality with the unpronounceable name appeared. My holiday spirit evaporated instantly. He was a Portuguese ringer for Ken Dodd! Slightly younger, certainly, but a Ken Dodd if ever I saw one. He had even rented the same teeth.

During the next two days, wherever we went in Funchal, we came face-to-face with the Iberian Doddy. He was obviously the greatest thing to hit Madeira since Henry the Navigator.

Friday dawned with its customary early sunshine. 'I can't stand those teeth another minute,' I complained to Joan. 'Let's go out of town today for an excursion somewhere. To the mountains perhaps?'

'You mean a *walk*?' she asked incredulously.

'I mean a *walk*,' I conceded.

Now it is not that I dislike walking. Not at all. If I really *have* to walk, I will. It is just something that I will not do out of choice. Joan, on the other hand, considers the worst thing to happen to civilization was the wheel. Speak the word 'intercontinental' and she instinctively reaches for her most comfortable shoes. 'Oh do come on,' she will chide, about the most arduous of journeys, 'it's only a *little* walk.' A 'little walk' to her, is anywhere she can reach before nightfall without either a packed lunch or an intravenous injection.

'I thought we could get a bus up the mountains and walk down,' I suggested. This made her half happy. Buses never usually figure in her walking schedules. 'Apart from anything else, it's safer,' I explained. 'If we are at the top of the mountain, we can look down at the town and see our route more clearly. If we walk *up*, we'll probably get lost.'

'Okay,' she agreed. 'But why don't we buy a book of levada walks? They sound great.'

I thought she had a point. I must confess (though not to her) the thought of these walks had intrigued me since our arrival on the island. Levadas are irrigation trenches of stone or concrete, usually about two feet wide and two feet deep, with a hard path on one side or the other. There are six hundred miles of these channels all over the island. Their advantage is that because they transport water, any incline tends to be gentle. In fact, the slope is often so slight, it can become illusory, with the walker convinced the flow is running uphill. Perhaps a bus trip up in the mountains and a leisurely zig-zag down, alongside those trickling waters, would be good therapy. Anyway, anything was better than the TV hype that was currently raging in Funchal.

Two hours later found us alighting from the yellow single-decker that had laboured so slowly for some four miles to the small mountain village of Monte. With much of the journey, even by road, being a one-in-three gradient, I was feeling pretty smug about my inspired itinerary. The bus stood panting for some minutes as if seeking its breath, before disappearing around a leafy bend in a cloud of diesel smoke. I nobly breathed the sharp mountain air, as Joan and I took off in the opposite direction.

'You do know the route, I hope?' she asked, with only slight anxiety.

'Of course I do. I even have the relevant page from the guide book, photostatted. Here, see for yourself.'

She studied it for a moment. 'Well I can't see any levadas around here.'

'Of course not,' I agreed. 'We have to seek them out. The map clearly states our route. All we have to do is follow it. Then, after some forty minutes, we will pick up the levada. We will meander down into town. In time for tea for you and a pint for me . . . easy.'

It was two hours into our forty-minute walk that doubt set in.

'Of course, you know the problem with this map, don't you?' I asked irritably.

'It's in English?' she asked.

'It doesn't register *distances*. It gives *times*. It says daft things like "After twenty minutes you will come to a fork in the path." That takes absolutely no account whatever of *you* stopping for a quarter of an hour to admire the view.'

'So you're saying we're lost?'

'I'm saying we're lost.'

'So what do we do now?'

'Well, we get rid of this bloody map for a start!' I pointed ahead, along the narrow path that circuited the curve of the ravine. 'If you look over the slope of that mountainside, you can just about see the sea.'

'And then what?'

'That tells us where the coast is. All we have to do then is follow the sea back to town. It can't be too far . . . and we must come out somewhere,' I added hopefully. Must-come-out-somewhere is probably the most commonly-used, self-deceiving phrase uttered by city-dwellers who are lost in the countryside.

In town, one always comes-out-somewhere. But in the countryside, *somewhere* tends to be *nowhere* – and in *someone else's* country, just two fields off the main road is the upper reaches of the Orinoco. The fact that our walk was to be considerably longer brightened Joan greatly as she cheerfully fell in behind.

Our main problem was that we were dressed for the sunny coast but the temperature had fallen rapidly, as indeed it frequently does in Madeira. Shorts, sun-hat, tee-shirt and dark glasses are not commonly found in a mountain survival kit. To make matters worse, the terrain had now changed. The path had become even narrower, the mountainside even steeper, and the slopes both above and below our path more and more entangled with small trees and undergrowth. They now looked almost impenetrable. It was the path or nothing. But most important of all, the direction of the path had slowly eased away from the coast, and the sea was no longer visible.

We plodded on for a further fifteen to twenty minutes and I had mentally switched my brain to neutral. I was looking, without necessarily seeing.

Suddenly Joan's anxious tone cut sharply into my meditations. 'I assume you *are* going to stop?'

'Eh, stop? Why should – ' I stopped all right.

There, some twenty yards ahead and tethered by a length of thick rope tied to the base of its wicked looking horns, was a very large, angry-looking billy-goat. For some reason, I have never liked goats. I was even on the side of the troll who lived under the bridge and was always trying to eat them. Perhaps the goat sensed this. Anyway, for whatever reason, he reared on his hind legs, then, dropping on all fours, he lowered his head and charged. He did not seem amused. Within the shortest of distances, he was at full speed, but just a few feet from me the restraining rope tightened and wrenched him on to his side. He appeared even less amused.

Slowly struggling to his feet, he shook his head and after a short consideration, decided to go berserk. He leaped and bucked and bounced and was certainly one very angry goat. I had no idea what the other end of the rope was tethered to but unless it was a fairly hefty tree, I could see problems.

'Back off!' cried Joan. 'You're frightening it.'

'*I* am frightening *IT*?' I echoed. 'Well, isn't that a

coincidence? 'Cos that thing is scaring the shits out of me.'

After a few more tugs on the rope, the goat returned to his original spot on the path and stood, head lowered, glowering at me.

'I think we're all right for the moment,' I said without too much conviction. 'But heaven only knows what we do now.'

'Let's wait here for a while. He may go away,' she ventured.

'Go away! Go away! How can he "Go away", woman? He's got a bleedin' rope round his horns that'd secure a battleship. He's going nowhere. That is unless the rope comes away at the other end . . . then he's coming straight for us.'

'I knew you shouldn't have tormented him,' she sighed.

She certainly had a point about waiting there. Above all we needed to take stock. We sat in silence on the path with our legs dangling over the slope.

'I suppose we *could* go back,' I ventured. 'The only problem is, I am not at all sure I know the way and it's getting really cold now.'

'Tell you what,' she said brightly, as she rummaged into the small canvas shopping bag that is a permanent extension of her right arm. 'Have a boiled sweet.'

I must point out here, that my wife has a holiday fixation about boiled sweets. *Boot's* Boiled Sweets to be exact. In a tin and covered with a fine dusting of icing-sugar. She never dreams of eating them at home but a tin of boiled sweets has been the first item on her every holiday list since rationing ceased forty years ago. We only need to be five minutes out of Heathrow or Gatwick and out will come the eternal boiled sweets. Personally I think they are boring but I am always amazed at the reaction of complete strangers as she hands them around. 'Oh, boiled sweets – how lovely!'

Even the nationality of the recipient seems to make little difference. I swear that to date, I have heard 'Oh, boiled sweets – how lovely!' in close on forty languages and dialects. If I am on holiday when the world finally disintegrates, I expect the last words I hear will be 'Have a boiled sweet'.

'How about him?' I jerked my thumb in the direction of our adversary. 'Goats are supposed to eat anything . . . think he'd like one?'

She shook her head. 'No, I think that goat prefers people.'

'Pity the Madeiran Ken Dodd wasn't here then. Might've made us quits.'

'Don't be so wicked,' she scolded. 'It's no use you blaming El Doddo. This trip was entirely your idea . . . listen! Can you hear someone calling?'

'Well, if it's the Madeiran Mountain Rescue you'd better answer.'

'No, I'm serious. But I can't make out where it's coming from.'

Just then, I too heard a frail voice but, likewise, could not decipher the direction.

'Look!' she exclaimed. 'Up there . . . under that small tree. There's an old lady . . . she's waving to us!'

I followed her pointing finger and sure enough, some fifty yards up the steep slope, was a young sapling. Beneath its branches, clinging on with one hand, was certainly an *old* lady. In fact, an *extremely old* lady. Tossing the goat a boiled sweet, we climbed to our feet. The goat immediately reactivated. Whether this reactivation was from the excitement of our sudden movement, or from the sheer physical pleasure of a Boot's Boiled Sweet, I was not sure. The newcomer was signalling clearly to us to stay where we were. She had the palms of her hands widespread towards us and was pushing them slowly backward and forward as if to say settle and keep still. We settled and kept still.

Once sure of our immobility, the old woman stooped and appeared to rummage on the ground in front of her. Seconds later she straightened triumphantly.

'Good God!' exclaimed Joan. 'Just look what she's got in her hand!'

Even at that distance it looked sinister. It was a wickedly curved and gleaming sickle. Even from fifty yards it looked razor sharp. Giving one last wave, she turned and began to strike the largest branch of the sapling. After three blows she removed a springy bough some six feet in length, with side shoots and leaves fanning out like an old punishment birch. Then, sickle in one hand, bough in the other, she began to bump her way down the slope on her buttocks!

'I can't look,' Joan cried. 'She'll break her neck. She's seventy-five if she's a day and she's not holding on!'

Seventy-five she may have been, although I would have placed her nearer eighty. But if her age was uncertain, her appearance was not. She was quite the filthiest woman I had ever seen.

'It's Gagool!' I whispered.

'Who?'

'Gagool . . . the evil witch from *King Solomon's Mines*. If she taps you on the shoulder, they cart you off and chop you up.'

I had not read the book since I was at school, but she

was Gagool right enough. In fact she looked old enough to be the 1885 original. Joan, whose formative years had been spent in the cinema and not deep in Rider Haggard books, decided Gagool was actually the wicked witch from *The Wizard of Oz*.

'Has she got red shoes?' she whispered.

Stupidly, I found myself looking. Anyway, her footwear ruled her out of any MGM movie. She had a dirty run-down pair of traditional Madeiran mountain boots, which were so worn they looked like boots pretending to be shoes. Her stockings, which ended just below her knees, had less material than holes, whilst her dress gave the impression that any introduction to water would cause disintegration. This assumption was not just for the dress, it was also for the wearer. Finally came her face. Such a face! It had the texture of a well-worn dartboard – but the crowning feature was a tooth. A long, solitary yellow tooth, that crept up from her lower gum, past the closed top lip of her mouth, as if its ultimate goal was to kiss the tip of the pointed nose that curved down towards it.

By now she had bounced on to the path. Cackling away in Portuguese, she struggled to her feet. Although we could not understand a word, we could not take our eyes from her mouth. As she jabbered, her single tooth upped-and-downed about six times a second. Yet in spite of her ridiculous appearance, as she stood there with her branch and her sickle, I felt a real sense of intimidation.

'We . . . are . . . trying . . . to . . . get . . . by,' I needlessly explained.

Now most Madeirans can speak at least a smattering of English but Gagool could manage not a word. Which, of course, placed us on a par. Our Portuguese was as prolific as her English. Holding up the sickle in her left hand and the branch in her right, she faced us like a geriatric version of Britannia's grandmother. Again she gave a slight pushing gesture, to indicate immobility.

Once satisfied, she turned and eased her way towards the goat. At first the animal did not move but just looked suspiciously towards her. When some five to six feet away, she pounced. Using an energy I could not believe she possessed, she belaboured the creature about the head with the sapling branch. She did not use the sickle, but appeared to have it poised in reserve should she need to decapitate.

After the briefest of struggles, she drove the goat over the edge, but the rope, and above all the creature's natural sure-footedness, caused it to regain its balance some eight feet down the incline. There it remained, bleating a rather sad protest. Her task completed, she turned towards us. Bowing slightly, she signalled us through. The sickle and branch were still in her hands. The branch I could certainly live with, but I never took my eyes from the sickle.

'Should I give her a boiled sweet?' asked Joan, with no sense of occasion.

I suppose there is just the possibility that our saviour would have wished for nothing greater than a boiled sweet. Yet the sickle suggested to me that something more tangible should be in evidence. Gallantly allowing Joan to pass through first, I began to give some thought to the question of a gratuity. Having no great plan to stand within reach of that poised blade, whilst sorting out my currency, I fumbled frantically in my pocket for a Madeiran banknote. Spectacleless, I pulled one out and prayed it was not too high a denomination. I breathed in deep relief; it was a hundred escudos (approx. forty pence).

Gagool was ecstatic! She broke out into another torrent of babble and this time the tooth became just a yellow blur. For one horrendous moment I feared she was about to kiss me in gratitude. However, with a final gracious and condescending wave, I hastened around the next bend.

'Okay, okay. I know she wasn't *really* Gagool,' I conceded, 'but that doesn't explain just who the hell she was.'

'You know what I think she's doing right now?' asked Joan thoughtfully.

'Tell me.'

'I wouldn't mind betting she's hauled that goat back on to the path and nipped hell-bent up to her tree to catch another pair of silly sods.'

'Well, I don't think that's right . . . and even if it was I wouldn't care. For forty pence it was worth it.'

'Forty pence *and* a boiled sweet,' she corrected. 'It was forty pence for her and a boiled sweet for the goat . . . anyway, where to now, Batman? There's another path ahead.'

There was indeed another path ahead. In fact there were three. From having no choice, we now had too many.

'Well,' she said. 'You have the map. Which one?'

'I don't need a map to make this choice. The right-hand path will do.'

'What makes you so sure?'

'It's the only one that slopes down. That's good enough for me. No one ever reached sea-level climbing *up* a mountain.'

Owing to the mist, we had no idea how high we were, but we had been climbing steadily and sometimes quite steeply since leaving the bus and I was just about shattered. This seemed the best reason of all to descend. The path was wide and good underfoot. If we had not been so cold, if we had not been so hungry, if we could have seen where we were going, there is a strong possibility we might have enjoyed the next two hours. Instead, it was early afternoon when our spirits finally soared. For not only did the sun break through but our path led over a tiny stone bridge. At last! A levada! Sure enough, there it was, some two feet wide and gurgling merrily. I could not have been happier if it had been the source of the Nile, although I would have doubtless been warmer. Once over the bridge, the path curved sharply and became the stone-slabbed edge of the levada. We were on route at last!

I studied my map with renewed interest and, taking a few bearings, came quickly to a conclusion.

'Of course, there is still the slight problem that we're lost,' I announced soberly.

'Grant you that,' she conceded. 'But at least we're lost in the sunshine and it appears to be goat-free . . . Hey,' she said as an afterthought, 'now it's warmer, we won't meet crocodiles, will we?'

'Shouldn't think so,' I assured her. 'The Lesser Madeiran Croc that basks at the tops of mountains in twenty-four-inch streams is pretty much extinct.'

The weather was by now so pleasant that if we had had any food we would have had a picnic. Instead we continued to walk. Once more the terrain changed. The mountains had given way to hills and on some were scenes of cultivation. Joan was some three yards ahead of me when I felt a light tap on my left buttock. It was quickly followed by two more. My first thought was – the goat!

Then I quickly realized that with horns like that, he was never a 'tapper'. What, then? I wheeled around and at first saw nothing except the levada and the hill we had just passed. As I looked down, there in front of me was a small girl of some six or seven years. She was shoeless and wearing a tired-looking frock some two sizes too large for her. She was olive-skinned, with a quite lovely face and extremely pretty eyes. Under her right arm she carried what was obviously a bottle, although thoroughly wrapped in tissue. Her left hand was held open and extended. She was asking me for money!

I stopped and called to Joan.

'Where has the kid come from?' she naturally asked. 'I've seen nothing to indicate anyone lives around here. Have you?'

'Where . . . do . . . you . . . live?' we both mouthed.

The child's reply was to extend her hand still further. 'Mon . . . ney,' she wailed.

'What do we do with her?' asked Joan.

I shrugged. 'Just let her pass, I suppose. Judging by that bottle, she must be on her way home anyway. Don't give her any money though. I hate to see kids begging.'

'I know!' said Joan, snapping her fingers. 'How about a nice boiled sweet?'

With that, she was straight in the canvas bag and almost immediately rattling the tin under the child's nose. The girl looked quite puzzled until Joan removed the lid. Her face changed immediately.

'Ah, Bon-Bons! Bon-Bons!' she chuckled, promptly seizing four of them.

With that, she fell in behind me and clearly indicated that the three of us should resume our walk.

Some ten minutes after the child joined us, she tapped

me once again and pointed to a small group of trees about a quarter of a mile ahead. Amongst the branches I could just see the outline of an old shed.

'Momma, Poppa,' said the girl proudly.

The route of the levada would take us within a few feet of the structure. The place itself appeared to have been squatted. Nothing about it seemed permanent, except perhaps a scruffy, stocky man of some thirty years, who lay sprawling drunk in a chicken pen. This, I assumed, was Poppa, doubtless to be the recipient of the bottle. Momma was hanging a line of children's washing but stopped and turned towards us. She was plump-to-fat and also aged about thirty years. She had a lovely round open face, such as some fat people are blessed with. She smiled and nodded as we neared. With the amount of small clothing on her sagging line, I was surprised not to see other children. Our young companion jumped from the levada path and ran to join the woman.

'Well, at least the area is inhabited,' I said, as we strode on.

'Don't you think we should have asked her the way back to Funchal?' asked Joan.

'I did think about it, but I couldn't help feeling that if Poppa woke, we could well have experienced a slight delay. I couldn't see you buying him off with a boiled sweet.'

Suddenly the now familiar tapping on my buttock began. There once more was the girl, and once more I had not heard her approach. This time she stretched out both hands.

'Momma, Bon-Bons . . . Momma?' she pleaded.

'She wants sweets for her mum,' I called.

Shaking her head in disapproval, Joan reluctantly meted out two more sweets.

'Bon-Bons! Bon-Bons! Poppa!' the girl insisted.

'No, you've had enough,' Joan scolded. 'Off you go.' She pointed her towards the shack. Without argument, the child ran off.

By this time, the levada was following the west side of a dried river valley. The valley was some six hundred yards across and a small stream, just a yard or so wide, could be discerned in its centre. Our path, which still edged the levada, was some hundred feet up from the valley floor.

'I wish I could see which way that stream is running,' I said wistfully. 'At least I would know if we are heading in the right direction.'

What was causing me some alarm, however, was the fact that the slope was falling away sharply from our path. A few minutes earlier, our little girl had been able to hop off. Now it was almost a sheer drop of a hundred feet. In addition, our path seemed to be narrowing.

'I'm not sure I want to go on,' said Joan worriedly. 'It looks quite dangerous.'

'Stay here and I'll go a little further. Perhaps it'll get better around the next bend.'

I left her sitting on the edge and enjoying what was at least a fine view. There was most certainly a change in the geography of the slope around that bend. Unfortunately, it was for the worse, the final straw being when both levada and path disappeared into a hole in the cliff face. A hole that could scarce have taken a medium-sized lizard, never mind me in my sun-hat. I was beginning to think El Doddo might well have been bearable after all.

Retracing my steps, not easily I may add, I was

announcing to Joan with false bonhomie, 'It's plan "B" I'm afraid. The levada's just vanished up its own – ' when I realized her attention was elsewhere. She glanced up for a moment, then seeing me, pointed down into the valley. I peered over the edge and for the first time noticed a path leading up to us from the valley floor. It was not an easy path by any means but nevertheless it was a path and three figures were laboriously climbing it. Somehow we had missed them on our original reconnaissance.

'Who are they?' I asked.

She shrugged. 'I can't really tell from this distance, except that they're two women and a fellah.'

'Well, if it's Ken Dodd, let's roll rocks down on him and sod off!'

'No such luck,' she said as they neared.

We moved to the side of the path and soon were able to assist the trio of newcomers up over the edge. I was delighted and not a little relieved to discover they were English! Not only were they the correct nationality but they also knew where they – and more importantly, we – were! I felt I had just discovered Livingstone.

It appeared our new acquaintances were also on a levada walk. Either their map was better or they were more intelligent, whatever. They had passed the squatters' shack and been beseiged by a horde of kids and a drunken man demanding money. They had been so distressed by this that they had sought to return by a different route. They had descended into the valley, hoping to follow the stream down to the coast road where, they assured us, a bus passed every forty minutes! Hurrah! The stream had proved too rocky for them and, because of being English I suppose, they had decided to return and brave out the bushwhacking squatters.

'Do have a boiled sweet,' offered Joan, as they finished their tale.

'Oh, boiled sweets – how lovely!' they chorused.

Our trio told us there was a simple way back to the coast, although there was no alternative to passing the squatters' shack. We therefore decided to form a convoy, with me in the rear, with sole responsibility for the boiled sweets. As we neared the shack, I could see all of the children we had not seen before. Poppa had now roused himself sufficiently to sit up. They came flooding to meet us. 'Bon-Bons! Bon-Bons!' they cried and to the astonishment of our threesome, 'Mon . . . ney' was not mentioned once. I doled out the sweets one at a time and at twenty-five-yard intervals, and after half a mile or so, the last of our appellants returned home.

We soon reached the place where we were to leave the levada, and once through some bushes, the bleached white road lay out welcomingly before us. Our friends were heading in the opposite direction, so before we took our leave, Joan, rather too generously I thought, offered one last dive into the multi-coloured tin.

'Now wait a minute,' I cut in. 'Let's get our priorities right. We have six sweets and ten days' holiday remaining. I refuse to face the unknown on this island again with anything less.'

Our bus arrived first. Waving a farewell, we climbed aboard. This was not easy, it was packed to the roof.

'Why so full?' I asked the conductor, whose English was excellent.

'Beeg show in town tonight, sur. "Eet's A Knockout". Everyone go.'

I closed my eyes in disappointment. I had a gut feeling that six boiled sweets were going to be totally inadequate.

'You know,' murmured Joan thoughtfully. 'This has not been a good day for you, has it? You've been haunted by Ken Dodd, you've probably walked further than you've ever walked before in your life. And I now have an additional piece of bad news. Want to hear it?'

'Shoot.'

'Well, when your three-year-old grandson is a little older and you're shooting him a line, like telling him what a brave soldier and policeman you once were, I am going to tell him about the day that you paid an old lady forty pence protection-money to fight a goat . . . fancy a boiled sweet?'

A Quick Punt up the Nile

'I must tell you now,' said Joan firmly, as she noticed me studying the brochure, 'I am not going to Egypt and that's final.'

'Why?'

'It's too hot . . . and besides . . . well, I've heard funny stories about the place.'

'Well, I know it's hot, but then no one goes to Egypt to lay in the sun, do they? In any case, what are these funny stories that bother you? Do you mean jokes? Or perhaps limericks? "There was a young lady from Cairo, who could do strange things with a Biro. It soon came to pass, with a pen up – " '

'That's it, thank you very much! I do not wish to hear any more. You can keep your disgusting army humour to yourself.'

'Look, it wasn't disgusting and it wasn't army humour. In fact it comes from the Job Centre and it's about a lady who had a novel way of cashing her giro.'

'I don't care – and I still don't want to go to Egypt.'

'But you still haven't explained the stories.'

She sighed. 'Look, when I left school at the end of the war, there was a bloke at the factory who had just returned from Egypt and I overheard him telling the engineers about it . . . and I tell you . . . it wasn't nice.

Besides,' she added with a shudder, 'I can't stand squiggly things that live in deserts.'

'You mean Arabs?'

'You know perfectly well what I mean. If you want to go, fine. But just go on your own because I'm sitting this one out.'

It was as a direct result of that conversation that I found myself alone at Heathrow for the afternoon flight to Cairo.

Now I would not like it to be thought that I cannot manage without a drink but on discovering Egyptian airlines, together with many of their hotels, are 'dry', I decided to purchase a three-bottle case of good quality Chardonnay in the duty-free at the airport. My flight had actually been called when I realized that even the best of wine is of little use without a corkscrew. If the sprint to the lounge shop did not take my breath away, the ludicrous price for a 'Souvenir of London' corkscrew certainly did. If the idea of this expensive junk was to remind some nostalgic foreigner of the memorable holiday he had just experienced in London, then I guess it was a success. Because mine snapped the moment it met the cork. We may have been 20,000 feet up and crossing the Loire but I instantly thought of London, for the understandable reason that I wished swiftly to return and smash the person who sold it me.

What I have noticed most about these irritations when travelling is their tendency to multiply.

'Have you tried pushing it into the bottle?' asked the fellow in the next seat. 'If you are persistent it does work . . . er, eventually,' he added, as a prophetic afterthought.

I think we were somewhere over the Adriatic when I

finally won. If 'won' could be classified as the correct term. Oh, I pushed it in right enough. The trouble was that I had savaged and mauled the bottle so much that its original chill was by then about ten degrees above body temperature. In fact it felt more like bean and lentil soup than a decent burgundy. The final velocity of the cork met the wine with such a force that it caused it to spit out to a truly amazing distance over a bewildering variety of objects. Including, I am delighted to say, the cretin who suggested the method to me in the first place. It did not even end there. I also twisted my left index finger so agonizingly that it is not right to this day.

Once I had sponged the wine from my trousers, navel and nose, I began to muse on the trip. Joan's 'funny story' reference had intrigued me at first, but after a while I believed I knew its content.

At the end of the war, I too had worked in a factory. Like her I had listened (with unquestionably greater enthusiasm) to the returning soldiers' tales. Later, when in the army myself, I would run across old Egyptian campaigners who would gleefully recount an incident they assured me they had seen in Cairo/ Port Said/ Alexandria or any of a cluster of towns and cities that tightly hugged the banks of the Nile. Each would give a lurid first-hand account of his intimate recollections. I must honestly say that even at fourteen years of age I was dubious. Everything I heard later in life merely increased that suspicion.

As late as the week before my flight, I attended a station reunion where I met some half-dozen former colleagues who had also served in the Middle East. 'Going to Egypt are you?' They would then nudge me confidentially. 'Well I'll tell you what you should be looking out for . . . and it ain't the bleedin' sphinx!' So it went on.

The incident, occasion or happening to which they referred, must, judging by the wide variations of date, have taken place outside time itself. The two players in the drama consisted of a nubile young maiden and an unusually attentive and incredibly endowed Arab donkey, who performed astonishing feats of copulation upon a raised stage.

Now as far as I could ascertain, judging by the wide time-span of these reported sightings, our nubile young lady had to be going on sixty-two. Which, considering the life she had led, to say nothing of the genital size of the average Arab donkey, was pretty good going. Either that, or there was a long line of Egyptian maidens doing little else but performing erotic gyrations with an equally impressive supply of randy donkeys. I had definite doubts.

The five-hour flight, plus the time difference, meant it was evening before we landed in Cairo. I had of course heard the term 'seething masses' before but until arriving in Cairo I am not sure I fully understood its significance. It even began at the airport, when I was just amazed that any guide could find us, claim us and then transport us safely and intact to our hotel. (This seemed not such an impressive feat when I later discovered that Cairo was, in fact, one of the safest cities in the world. Apart from the threat of being permanently surrounded by fornicating donkeys, I was also assured that I would lose even the very laces from my shoes whilst I watched. Another army myth?)

The greatest problem for the tourist in Egypt is time. There is never enough of it. I think I spent the whole holiday in a state of permanent wonderment. It began early next morning on the statutory trip to the sphinx and the pyramids. At first, Philistine that I am, I was indifferent to the idea. I had not come to Egypt for this. I had already seen the pyramids in a thousand films, newsreels and pictures. For me they were clichéd, hackneyed, overrated and as familiar as Battersea Power Station. They were a tourist trap that I wanted little to do with. Okay, so the tour included them. Fortunately it was the first morning, so at least it was soon over and done with. Wow! What a prat!

My conversion took as long as the descent of four bus steps. As I dropped into the lung-searing heat and looked around me, I was hooked. 'Everyone fears time,' the Egyptians say. 'But even time fears the pyramids.' And with every reason I would say. Their size; their mystery; their silence! They are like three mute giants who see, hear, yet say nothing. Their treasures are not what they hide but what they know. Pharoahs, Kings and package-tourers hold them in the same awe and reverence and are equal before them. Yes, unquestionably a prat.

Perhaps the euphoria that breaks over visitors causes a blank to appear in their minds. Could be, I suppose. But nature, abhorring a vacuum, swiftly fills this momentary void with something that has evolved with the pyramids themselves – camel owners! They catch you at your highest state, when earthly things no longer seem to matter. The amazing thing is that this takes place in a desert, with little or no cover. Yet I never saw them arrive. I stepped off the bus, marvelled, gave a deep sigh and the next thing I knew I was sitting on a camel, and a bad-tempered smelly brute he was too. Not only that, but I had a turban on my head and the camel owner had already taken four snaps of me with my own camera that was set for three metres, indoors, with flash! As someone who uses one roll of film for every three holidays, I found this criminally extravagant. Apart from anything else, T.E. Lawrence was the only European who ever looked anything but a total idiot on the back of a camel. The last thing I needed was four photographs as permanent reminders.

Later, when I was finally off the beast, I watched these operators with a new group of tourists. Even the most observant of these newcomers still found themselves turbaned and marooned astride the most uncomfortable creature since the brontosauras. One thing was sure. I now knew why those insatiable Egyptian maidens chose a donkey. It was because they couldn't stand the breath of a camel. At ten paces it can disintegrate rocks. So if 'Time fears the pyramids' then the pyramids must be worried sick over the camels.

Our touring group was, as far as most groups go, rather small. There can be as many as forty people on some tours. I find them unwieldy and lacking in cohesion. We were about twenty-six in number and luckily the chemistry was excellent from the start. This was always a marvellous piece of luck. Few tours are ever in open warfare but certainly some harmonize better than others.

We were a fairly cosmopolitan bunch and I was surprised how many Antipodeans were with us. Perhaps because they seem so remote from the rest of the world, both Australians and New Zealanders do tend to save up for that grand long tour that may include all Europe, Asia or sometimes both Americas. If they save extra hard, they will occasionally do the whole world! Many of these tours will have Egypt as either the last port of call, or as an extra thrown in before that last, long journey home.

Probably everyone's favourites on the tour were Dick and Henrietta. They were real chalk and cheese. Henrietta was what Joan would call a real lady. She was in her late sixties, slimly built, always immaculately dressed, did nothing at speed and wore white gloves at all times. She had, to use her own expression, 'summered in England', taking in such bunfights as Henley, Glyndebourne, Wimbledon and a Royal Garden Party. And I would not mind betting that if she was not actually presenting the prizes, she would have a front row seat at each. She was, to my total astonishment, Australian and had been all her life. Yet I would have placed her no nearer Australia than Cheltenham. To even share a seat with her on the bus was like being granted an audience with Marie Antoinette. I always felt deeply humble for the next twenty minutes.

Dick, on the other hand, was a complete opposite. Well, perhaps not *totally* complete. There was certainly the same moneyed background but that, plus their gender, was the only thing they had in common, for Dick was also a lady. Perhaps not the Henley and Glyndebourne type, more the 'I'll-go-up-the-Congo-and-find-its-bloody-source' type. Although we loved her dearly, she *did* look a little like Olive Oyl in the Popeye cartoons. She was also nearly seventy and had promised herself she would travel every country in the world on her own. With the exception of Rumania, she had accomplished it. As opposed to Henrietta, she travelled light. With her overnight holdall, a jar of Fortnum and Mason's marmalade and a hundred tea-bags, she would take on the world – had, in fact. She had been born in England but had left for New Zealand before she was ten.

'But why are you called Dick?' we obviously asked.

'My name is really Beatrice, but I ask you, do I look a Beatrice?'

We had to agree with her. If it was a choice between Dick and Beatrice, then it was Dick every time.

'You see, my father wanted a boy who could play cricket for Surrey. Well, he didn't have one. I was about as close as he could get. So he called me Dick. It just sort of stuck. I don't mind it really, I've answered to it for most of my life.'

This 'travelling light' certainly had advantages but her clothes of course were of necessity, limited. As a result of this, within minutes of checking in at a hotel, she could usually be spotted scuttling around the garden in her liberty-bodice looking for a suitable bush on which to dry her intimates.

It was quite early in the tour that the mystery of the acrobatic donkeys was solved. A few of us were having a drink in the hotel bar one evening when the subject was surprisingly broached. Even more surprisingly, by Henrietta! Her source, some returning 1945 military, had been the same as the three others in the group who had also heard of the equine Errol Flynn.

'I don't believe it, my dear, do you?' she asked a group in general.

We all agreed in unison but deep down felt we would be happier with more visual proof.

'I mean,' she continued, 'it's biologically quite impossible, quite impossible.'

'Well,' sighed Ken, a builder from Yorkshire, who stood shaking his head, ''e'd certainly be worth a bob or two in cloobs around Batley, I can tell thee.'

Next morning at Giza, a local guide was explaining the hieroglyphics on the well-preserved wall of a tomb. His audience consisted of our group plus fifty or so other visitors. These picture-words filled the entire space from left to right and top to bottom. However, the light did not clearly reach the top fifteen inches or so, near the ceiling. The guide explained everything we could see in great detail. Then Henrietta sidled up to me. Her gloved hand rested on my left shoulder as she applied the gentlest of pressure to bend my ear down to her mouth.

'If you look carefully at the darker strip near the top of the wall, my dear, you may learn something of interest,' she whispered. She moved quickly and smoothly to other members of our group and I assume her dialogue was the same, because on her departure, each squinted up at the gloom. She was right! There in stone carvings, several millennia old, was a whole pageant of donkeys and maidens – and it certainly wasn't carrots we could see.

'Can you explain the hieroglyphics at the top for us please?' asked Henrietta of the guide, in the sweetest of tones.

It was not as if he refused to answer. He simply seemed to put on a invisible shell as if he hadn't heard the question. She asked twice more. Twice more he did not hear. Finally even Henrietta got the message.

Two days later, she repeated the question at another tomb to a different guide but the result was the same. We began to realize that if you looked hard enough, these bi-species couplings were all over the place. They must either have held some deep religious significance for the tomb-makers, or they were the work of some early dynastic, highly imaginative stone-mason, carving out the world's first graffiti.

'Yer know, I reckon wi' cracked it,' said Ken thoughtfully. 'Tha' weren't nae *real* fornication at all. All that them boggers saw, when they were here in t'army, were bludy carvins! Eet's bin passed on from one t'other until eet's now some bludy Gippo myth.'

'And so it should be,' said another of the group. 'That

surely is what Egypt is all about . . . myths. Sun Gods, Boy Kings, Ram-headed princes! Well, I for one am going to believe every detail of it – so there.'

'Well, I can't help feeling a bit let down,' said Henrietta sadly. 'I was quite looking forward to that part of the tour.'

I studied her for a moment. I was beginning to see her in a new light. It is true I could not actually visualize her standing on a chair at the local 'Hen night' yelling 'Git 'em orf!' at the male stripper, but there was definitely more to this lady than gentility and white gloves.

From the point of view of the present-day traveller, trying to 'do' the country in a fortnight, it is difficult to say what is the real core of ancient Egypt. Marvels in one shape or another seem to be everywhere. But if one *had* to pick a single spot, then arguably it would have to be Luxor. With its Valley of the Queens, the Valley of the Kings and the stunning majesty of Karnak, it simply has to win, even over such jewels as the pyramids at Giza and the temple at Abu Simbel. There are three ways the tourist travels there from Cairo. Either by boat, plane or train. The boat sounds fine but 400 miles of river can take a sizable chunk of a two-week holiday. The plane is certainly quick but somehow removed from the very purpose of your trip. That leaves us with the train, which in this case was the overnight Cairo-to-Luxor sleeper. That very phrase, 'overnight Cairo-to-Luxor sleeper', had sold me the tour in the first place. It sounded so exotic. Throughout my life I seem to have seen films set in sleeper-trains and I had always longed to try them. Be it the intrigues on the Orient Express, the adventures on the Canadian Pacific or just the spy train in *The Lady Vanishes*, I had been fascinated by them all. Well now, here it was, Cairo-to-Luxor! I was going aboard and hugging myself with pleasure.

Perhaps it is possible to look forward *too* much to something. Whether I felt I needed the cigar-smelling, solid mahogany of the Orient Express or the fragrant softness of Marilyn Monroe's sleeper in *Some Like It Hot*, I am not sure, but reality was most certainly different. First problem was the space – or more accurately, no space. I had seen larger tortoises. Yet in comparison to most, I was fortunate, because although I was travelling solo, I had a twin compartment. I am not large, but heaven only knows how two people manage in such an area, especially if they are even faintly cuddly.

I spent an hour planning how I would sleep. I was pondering the chances of removing the window, when the attendant arrived with dinner and a couple of beers. He lifted a flap here, pulled something out there, and then, swivelling the whole lot around, set the meal before me. I was obviously supposed to be impressed. I wasn't. It was like having a lap-dinner riding pillion on a motor-bike. Forty minutes later the attendant returned. He dropped *down* a flap here, pushed something *in* there and kicked the whole caboodle into an entirely new shape. This promptly transformed my compartment from a tiny uncomfortable dining-room, into an even tinier, more uncomfortable bedroom.

It was around this stage that the magic really began to fade. Firstly, it was a bit lonely. Yet one can hardly play the benevolent host in an Egyptian sleeping-compartment. With just three people standing, intimacy would certainly occur. It would be the only way to move about.

The second problem was the train itself. I can only

assume that much of the line is single-track, because we were shunted several times into some sort of lay-by. There we would stop momentarily whilst another train roared past in the opposite direction. This meant the train did an awful lot of stopping, starting and swaying around. Finally, but not out of choice, I went to bed.

Usually, after a three-course meal and a couple of beers, the one thing I would *not* do is lie down. Even if I did I would ensure I was totally immobile. Just about the last thing I would do is jerk backward, forward and roll around. But on this train, jerking backward, forward and rolling around was a statutory obligation. Biology not being my strong point, I am unsure as to the exact position of my stomach. But I had this worrying feeling that it should have been more than four inches below my chin. The only good thing about this rogue intestine was that it made no further attempt to climb higher. Instead it just lay there for the next twelve hours, slurping, bubbling and rumbling.

I realized there were questions to be answered. Namely, what had happened to the exotic magic I was expecting? Where was that air of good living and affluence I had seen in so many train films? I don't remember James Bond throwing up in *From Russia with Love*. So why did I feel so bloody awful? Of course, in situations like these and particularly on your own, you do tend to become selfish. My main worry was that I would die. Now although I had no particular plans for my eventual demise, being carried off by a couple of beers and an Egyptian lamb casserole somehow lacked class.

It was next morning before I discovered others had similarly suffered. One young couple, being unable to sleep, decided upon the time-honoured way of utilizing their nocturnal sleepless intervals. In addition, this activity also had the advantage of saving space. After all, one person on top of another certainly makes for more room in the rest of the compartment. It says a considerable amount for their dedication that even when the train eased into yet another lay-by, they were still engaged on this space-saving exercise. His enthusiasm waned a little when she tapped him on the shoulder to whisper that the lay-by was in fact a station platform. He anxiously peered over his shoulder at the three female faces who were, in turn, peering studiously down at his bum. The three faces may have been closely veiled but he claimed the six eyes were certainly wide open.

As I listened to the experiences of the rest of the party, I immediately decided upon my travel plan for the return to Cairo a few nights later. I was to stick to this plan and it worked beautifully. Firstly, I dispensed completely with dinner. Lamb casserole and the local beer were out. I simply ordered a bread roll and a bottle of cheap, dark red Egyptian plonk. This has three advantages. It kills mosquitos, tranquillizes rhinos and nullifies every sound between Luxor and Cairo. At five minutes past eight in the evening, I placed my weary head on the hard pillow of my tiny bed.

At ten minutes past eight next morning, I was shaken awake by one of our Australian girls who had feared for my safety after receiving no response to a severe door-pounding. I was still in a semi-trance when we alighted from the train in Cairo. I believe the sleeping-car attendant had found my appearance a little disconcerting. Well, stuff him. I had had my best sleep in years.

Our hotel was beautifully situated on an island in the Nile.

I seemed to spend every minute in Luxor in complete wonderment. We became almost sated as we saw what appeared to be one miracle after another. 'How on earth did they do this?' we would ask a dozen times a day. A guide put forward a theory to me that I had never heard before. I must say it sounded as plausible as any other I had experienced. I had always been led to believe that these enormous ancient Egyptian projects had been built by slaves – or subjects so ruled that they might as well have been slaves. But the guide put forward almost the opposite theory. 'Could slaves accomplish such incredible work?' he asked. 'This was surely a work of love?'

At times the heat is unbearable. (On our visit to the Valley of Queens for example, the thermometer showed 126° Fahrenheit.) Forced labour in these circumstances, with little or no medical knowledge, must be genocidal. He suggested that the whole population took part, primarily as an act of worship. Because of the regular flooding of the Nile, there were several months each year when the land could not be worked. He also explained that the pharaohs were thought of as gods. Therefore, each year, almost the entire population of the country gave around three months to whatever project was being undertaken at the time. As my knowledge of Egyptology consists entirely of Boris Karloff's black and white version of *The Mummy's Curse*, I was a receptive audience.

Incidentally, this obsession horror-film makers have with ancient Egypt may not be as illogical as we sometimes believe. One of the few bills found for the cost of the pyramids relates not to gold, silver or iron but to horseradish, onion and garlic! Perhaps one can sense here the origin of the maidens' preferences for donkeys?

One of the biggest miracles of Luxor had to be Karnak.

The Great Temple of Amon, for example, contains 134 columns, each about eighty feet tall. What will not be shown in any guide book, however, is that these columns are haunted. No, not by a pre-dynastic being, nor even a common-or-garden mummy. They are haunted by a bewildered old Arab with a shiny new camera. He appeared time and time again, asking our group to pose whilst he meticulously arranged his camera. This took ages.

We had no idea *why* he wanted these pictures, for he never spoke a word. He just smiled helplessly and waved his hands to indicate to us to open out or close in. Once everyone was in position, he would peep through the viewer. He would then discover that one of the many buttons, switches or levers was not correctly set. Lifting his head, he would smile an apology and readjust. By this time at least one of us would have moved. Once more he would stretch out his hands, once more he would readjust.

We must have gone through this procedure some half-dozen times in an hour. I had the feeling he had acquired the camera that very morning, together with one crash-course lesson in its workings. If so, he could not have been paying attention. He had such a kindly face that no one wished to offend him, although we certainly wished to avoid him. The following morning, as we boarded our bus, he came running down the road with an armful of photographs. We realized then he must have been a 'street' photographer on his first assignment.

If his photography was bad, his system was appalling. He had dozens of assorted groups, mostly just heads but always with masses and masses of blurred, blue sky. The fondest mother would not have recognized her only son, even if he had been able to get into the picture in the first place. Predictably, he never sold one photograph. I felt so unhappy for him, I was tempted by buy at least two skies.

'No, no,' forbade our guide severely. 'We must not encourage inferior work. He must understand he must improve.'

'Poor sod,' murmured Henrietta sadly, 'but you do wonder how they built the pyramids.'

On the last evening of our stay in Luxor, we were invited to join the festivities at a Nubian village a short distance down the Nile. Some sixty people from the hotel were due to board three small feluccas that were scheduled to leave the hotel jetty at 6 p.m. On our arrival at the jetty, we were each given a long cotton garment that reached down to our ankles. I must say the ladies' cloaks, which were in the palest of greens, were almost elegant. The same could not be said for the men's. For elegant, read elongated; for cloak, read nightshirt. Nevertheless, everyone entered into the spirit of the thing and most raced back to their hotel room to change into their new garb. There was the usual predictable hilarity as we pointed at each other, doing and saying all the silly things that people do and say under such circumstances.

Then we stepped into the boats for the short journey down the east bank. The boats had a white canvas awning stretched across their whole width, just a little above head height. This was to keep out the sun in the heat of the day. They also had a sailing mast but the sails were folded. Forward movement was generated by a jet-black Nubian standing in the stern using a long pole, as if in a punt. It was obvious from this that we would be sticking to the shallows near the bank. There had been a slight delay in the departure of our felucca, seemingly because of the non-arrival of our 'punter'.

After a few minutes, a smiling young boy about fifteen years old appeared and we were pushed from the hotel jetty by a member of the staff. The scene seemed particularly peaceful. The water was as still as glass, and now that we had come to terms with our somewhat ludicrous attire, our attention focused on other matters – especially the most incredible sunset. The huge crimson sun seemed to be setting so close that with a long pole I could have reached out and touched it. Perhaps someone on board tried, because a sudden yell drew our attention to the fact that our young Nubian had lost his pole. It was a tantalizing distance away – only inches out of reach. Within a minute or so it was *well* out of reach and we began to drift more and more towards the centre of the river.

'The sail!' called a voice. 'Put up the sail. We'll do it that way.'

Nervous giggling began and someone called to the other two boats, now some distance downstream. They slowly turned about, but because we were now well out of the shallows, their poles were not long enough to touch the riverbed. Knowing nothing of sailing, I was content to leave matters to those who did. It soon dawned on me that 'those who did know' did not know *much*, because if anything, our situation worsened. We were not simply drifting aimlessly, we were twirling round and round as if in an invisible whirlpool.

'It's the sheet, the canvas sunsheet,' called Dick. 'It's counteracting the sail. It'll need to come down.'

There was no shortage of help over this. Few of us could sail but we could all untie a few knots that held the sunsheet in place. We rushed to assist. There was a surfeit of help and an absence of plan. The result was that the bright white sunsheet promptly fell across the entire width of the felucca, draping itself over everyone. From the river-banks and the other two feluccas, it must have looked like a rapidly rotating ghost ship . . . a ghost ship with bumps.

As we struggled to throw back the sheet, the sheer lunacy of the situation struck me. 'Here, just a minute,' I said to Dick. 'Do you think perhaps this is one of the all-time wind-ups?'

'How?' she asked.

'Well, they've dressed us in nightshirts, cast us adrift on the Nile with a kid too small to hold a pole and finally spun us dizzy, wrapped in canvas. Stuff the Nubian village. At this rate we'll finish up in their cooking pot.'

She had by this time raised the sheet immediately above Henrietta to a height that at least allowed that lady some breathing-room (and she still appeared as unruffled as ever). As soon as I finished speaking, Dick burst into fits of laughter and was unable to hold up the covering. Henrietta was once more obliterated by a dozen square yards of canvas.

Minutes later, when the canvas was rolled back for the final time, Henrietta was revealed, sitting white-gloved, straight-backed and calm, with just the faintest of smiles, for all the world as if she were waiting for a late carriage for the opera.

I wondered how the Nubians would take to this daft pantomime. To the best of my knowledge, I had never before met one. I thought perhaps they would flee from us screaming or at least treat us with the smug, sneering tolerance of Spanish waiters. They did neither. Instead they acted as dignified hosts, just as if a roll-around-a-felucca was a significant religious ritual. But then they probably thought Henrietta was of royal blood. I certainly did.

Our trip to the Valley of the Queens coincided with our hottest day, although I daresay it is every tourist's hottest day. The sheer geography of the valley makes it a natural cauldron. We had just left the temple to Queen Hatshepsut and the landscape was barren rock and shimmering desert, without an inch of green in sight. Suddenly our bus stopped outside a rather rambling wooden shack. This building appeared to have no function. It was miles from anywhere and without a sign of life.

Our guide smiled, gestured us in and said, 'Refreshments'.

We were surprised, but would have certainly welcomed anything to drink, so dutifully we alighted and gradually we trooped in. We were met at the door by a short, tubby, genial middle-aged Egyptian with a smile as wide as his face. He led us to a large bare-boarded room that contained a bar and a list of assorted beverages. There was the usual demand from the girls for 'the ladies' and soon the customary queue formed. I had barely begun my beer when gales of laughter rose from the surprising direction of the ladies' lavatory. Apparently this loo was correct in every detail, even to the pull-chain. The problem was, the very location of the place ensured there would be no running water. Therefore, when the incumbent stood to pull the chain, nothing happened, except for the crash of the lever in the empty cistern. This crash was actually a signal, for suddenly our genial host would hurtle into the loo with a bucket of water.

Unfortunately, because of the heat, one of our Australian ladies decided to rinse her hair in cold water (something she did frequently throughout the tour). Seeing the bucket, she bent down and ducked her head into it and proceeded to shake it vigorously. Of course the question then arose, where did the water come from in the first place? Or even more importantly, what (or even whose) water was it? The two people in our group who had ordered tea promptly cancelled and the poor girl spent the remainder of the day sniffing suspiciously at her tresses.

'Well I thought you would have realized that,' said the experienced Dick. 'After all, you are in a desert. What did you expect to come flushing down – sand?'

Soon, as the holiday drew to a close, I realized how much easier it would be to tour Egypt if one did not sleep. There would be so much more time to see all those treasures and sights. This was best encapsulated on our last night when almost our entire group decided to go to a night-club together. We were due to leave for the airport at 5 a.m. the next morning. At 1 a.m. we had still not been served dinner.

'There you are,' said Dick cheerfully, as we staggered back to our rooms at 3 a.m. 'See how much there is to enjoy if you don't sleep?'

Strangely, it was not until the afternoon of that last full day in Cairo that I saw my most memorable sight. It was not a tomb, museum or a pyramid. It was not gold, silver or precious stone. It was not in the Valleys, on the Nile or against the majestic Aswan dam. It was simply a woman on a bus.

About a dozen of us had gone to a market to buy those last minute take-home presents. Or in my case, to window-shop. I am *not* a great present-buyer. I am not sure if it is meanness, or just a lack of enthusiasm.

Anyway, that day I went mainly for the ride. Because of the maze of identical streets and the masses of identical crowds, we arranged to meet opposite a tall mosque which was an easily-seen local landmark. Unusually for me, I arrived first, and to pass the time began to amuse myself by watching the local transport system. Or rather, the people using the transport system. It was impressive.

A single-decker bus would appear at the corner of the market, more or less empty. I would guess its seating capacity as around forty-seven. There would be no queue as we know it but a seething throng of people, far more people than had just alighted. It made no difference how large this crowd was, the bus would devour them all. I use the word *devour* deliberately, because that is exactly what it appeared to be doing. It was like a mass self-sacrifice, as if huge numbers of people had assembled around a quicksand at either end, then slowly eased themselves into it. One particularly large absorption had left me convinced that no living creature, however small, could gain an inch of space in the vehicle. This particular bus had been the most crowded by far, with arms and heads hanging gratefully from its open windows. I had by this time been joined by other members of our tour, and seeing my fascination, they joined me in people-watching.

'By heaven – luke!' called Ken excitedly. 'I do believe yon lass is tryin' t'get bus!'

We watched in disbelief as a svelte young figure dressed from head to toe in black, with just her eyes exposed, moved gracefully but quickly towards the rear door. It would have been an impressive feat for so slight a figure to have gained a foothold on even the first step. But it was not the girl herself who had caused our excitement – it was what she carried on her head. Her slender arms were raised to secure the balance of a large, oval-shaped zinc bath! It was the sort I grew up with and used to see in front of our fireplace every Friday night when I was a child.

'Bliddy hell!' exploded Ken. 'All the lass wants is a bliddy coal-miner sittin' in it wi' his cap on an' I'll reckon I'll have seen everythin'!'

'She's never going to get on,' I heard myself saying. 'Never in a million years is she.'

I was not sure what impressed me most, the girl or the passengers who were already on the bus. I was imagining the dialogue back home. 'Go on, sod off! Don't bring that bloody thing in here!' and as for our conductors – well! They would, by now, have been in a state of complete apoplexy. Slowly, oh so slowly, the girl eased herself into the bus entrance. First, half of her left leg. Then she bent gracefully at the knees and slowly inched the bath downward until it had the minutest of clearances. This was followed by a wiggle of hips, a thrust of thigh and suddenly she was in!

She was not only in but gone from sight, submerged totally into the human quicksand. I was still astonished that no one appeared to complain. Even the driver had sat patiently staring into his mirror, observing her progress. The bus sat so low on its springs that the wheels could barely be seen. At first, the burden appeared too much for the engine. It roared; then came a grinding of gears and a sudden lurch forward.

'If lass had watter in t'bath, there's a few in t'bus who'd be a bit cleaner reet now,' said Ken thoughtfully.

Eventually it gathered momentum and was soon lost in the mayhem that passes for Cairo traffic.

'You know,' said Dick sadly, 'that's the most impressive

thing I have seen in Egypt and not one of you buggers had a camera ready.'

The one consistent thing about these tours is that people will pass through your life for a couple of weeks and then be gone forever. Oh, certainly, people swop addresses, but in reality, they rarely see each other again. There was no point, for example, in swopping addresses with the antipodeans. My brother, who lives in Melbourne, would justifiably moan if my yearly letter became bi-annual, because I was writing to some fellow country-wench of his in the outback. (Come to think of it, Joan wouldn't be over the moon either.) It was with this philosophy in mind that we each made our farewells at the airport. We were a sensible bunch and not a name and address was exchanged. Dick, by far the most experienced traveller of us all, shook everyone warmly by the hand.

At first I thought it strange that she never spoke. Then, when she gripped my hand, I could easily see why. Her eyes were full of tears. The old softy! Every country except Rumania and she is still upset at a parting! There was no doubt her old Dad did her wrong. Cricket or no cricket, she was never a 'Dick'. She was truly a beautiful Beatrice.

Trish, Trash and Tangerine

I am convinced that some holidaymakers use their children like mines. I don't mean they float them in the pool, or explode them in sewers. Oh no, it is much more subtle than that. They simply scatter them innocently around the hotel complex, hoping some passing idiot will take a parental interest in their well-being. The child is something of a detonator. Once an inquisitive fellow-tourist is hooked, the offspring simply triggers the fuse . . . and presto! The most boring pair of adults you are ever likely to meet suddenly appear and explode their tedium over the rest of your holiday.

These parents will usually be from a suburb of east London, probably Dagenham, or Barking. For some reason you never discover, they are certainly not short of a few bob. Strangely enough, although they will tell you about practically everything else, they are oddly reticent about being so well fixed.

She will be a fleshy, stiff haired, back-combed blonde called 'Trish'. He will be a beer-bellied, slightly balding six-footer, with ludicrously long shorts, named 'Gal'. Her 'Trish' is not too difficult to decipher because she wears a gold necklace bearing a long name-tag with the letters TRICIA boldly inscribed. On the other hand, his 'Gal' is much more difficult. With no clues readily available, the complete indifference to his name becomes overriding. He therefore remains Gal for the rest of the holiday.

The children will be about eight and ten years old. 'Shal', the boy (alias Shane) will never stop eating or talking. Although words like 'I want', 'gimme' and 'won't' tumble freely from his lips, other words, such as 'please', 'thank you' and 'pardon' never rate a mention.

His eight (going on twenty-four-)-year-old sister, 'Leese' (gold name-tagged LISA), will almost be a saving grace. Precocious, certainly. Yet with a smile that can readily disarm. One could believe that she may yet have a childhood, if kept apart from the rest of the trio for the next ten years.

The Spanish Costas particularly are infested with Gals and Trishes. The experienced traveller therefore soon learns not to make the usual pleasantries to their off-spring. This is fine up to a point, yet it may still not be enough. Like a Wild-West marshal, one soon learns never to sit with one's back to the bar door. The evening you forget this practice will be the longest night of your holiday. First it will be the voice, the flat London suburban tone that makes boring points on 'Phone-ins'.

'Oh look! It's Uncle Harry! Hullo Uncle Harry. Say hullo to Uncle Harry then, gang.'

You groan inwardly and seek for a quick excuse to leave but your pint is only half finished.

'What've you been up to today then, you old rascal – no don't tell me, I'm too young to know! Ha Ha Ha! Don't mind if we join you, do you? No, come on, Shal . . . Leese, say hullo to Uncle Harry and Auntie Joan.'

Even before his last sentence is completed, my next

sentence has begun. The four of them have sat down and prepared themselves for a long stay.

This opening gambit of Gal's is doubly unfortunate. Apart from the dreary evening stretching ahead, there is the additional insistence of both moronic parents that their rotten kids call me 'Uncle'. To make matters even more infuriating, neither child ever does. But the parents, as if determined to set an example, hardly ever miss a breath with it. Perish the thought that anyone should think I am related to them. I am a *real* uncle twice over and have never felt the need for more. Pseudo-uncles have never appealed to me. Far too many of them finish up nicked for indecency.

'Look,' I said to Joan later, as I fell glaze-eyed on to the bed. 'That bloody family have our range. We seem destined to acquire them wherever we go, either in the hotel or the town.'

'Yes, Uncle Harry,' she mocked. 'So what do you propose to do about it?'

'Well, what we need is a break. We've had that quartet for a week now and I've got battle fatigue. How about going away for a couple of days – let some other poor sods have them?'

'A break? Are you serious? You're on holiday, man! How can you have a break when you're supposed to be on holiday?'

'I've seen this poster, down by reception. It's for an overnight stay in Tangier. Leave 8 a.m. Tuesday, back 4 p.m. Wednesday. How about it?' I persisted.

'How about what?'

'Tangier, woman! Tangier! Do you want to go or not?'

'Where is it and how do we get there?'

'It's just across the Gibraltar straits, on the northern

tip of Africa. We get a coach to Algeciras and a ferry across the mouth of the Mediterranean . . . you know, your geography is *appalling*. Fancy not knowing where Tangier is!'

'You forget, I was a war baby. How about snakes?'

'What about them?'

'Well, are there any? You know I don't like snakes and you did say it was Africa.'

'Yes, but it's not the bleedin' Congo! I mean, it's only *just* in Africa. It is simply a port on the Moroccan coast. Probably more like Barnstaple if the truth be known.'

'Well . . . okay,' she conceded grudgingly. 'But only if you're sure there are no snakes.'

'Good. I'll book first thing tomorrow. I'm sure you'll enjoy it.'

I experienced just a twinge of conscience about my snake denial, primarily because the poster that had attracted my eye in the first place did so by portraying an Arab snake-charmer, sitting on his haunches, playing his flute to a wicked-looking cobra. The snake was swaying just in front of him – reminiscent of the leading lady when they used to make films about trumpet players.

We had a day to spare before our trip – or 'safari', as Joan insisted on calling it. I had a worried feeling she would appear that morning wearing a pith helmet and four yards of mosquito netting. To avoid the fearsome foursome, we had decided to spend a day in the foothills that lay in the opposite direction to our seashore hotel. In order to do this, we needed to cross the dreaded coast road that hugs the Costa Del Sol. This is a highway that has seen off as many Spaniards as the Civil War. Even to give the *appearance* of crossing the thing is enough to inspire a cacophony of car horns. So it was no great surprise when one passing taxi played a persistent and irritating medley.

What *was* a surprise, however, was that it stopped and we recognized both passengers. Derek and Josie Blake had been friends of ours for years and were now on a helpful errand for a neighbour back home in London. They were in the last day of a holiday near Malaga, and because of their location were taking the taxi to a distant village, to where a neighbour had thoughts of purchasing a holiday flat. They were, in effect, giving it the once-over so they could report back before the prospective purchaser became too committed. We spent a few 'Oh-what-are-you-doing-here?' minutes before accepting their invitation to join them in their search.

After some thirty minutes, we turned off the road down a pot-holed dusty lane that led, according to the estate agent's description, to an idyllic Iberian fishing village. Well, fishing village it was, Iberian it was. Idyllic it was *not*. In fact, our first impressions were of an unstaffed council tip.

'El centro?' asked the wavering Derek.

'El centro,' assured the greasy driver.

Alighting on to a dried mud and cobble pavement, we looked around. It was empty. We had, of course, forgotten that siesta was still very much practised away from the usual tourist traps – and this village was certainly *never* going to be a tourist trap.

'I bet we're the first strangers in town since Hannibal,' muttered Derek disenchantedly.

'True,' said Joan, as she nodded towards a few deposits in the middle of the lane, ' – and they haven't cleared up yet after the elephants.'

Derek paid off the cab driver who sped away quickly in a cloud of dust that billowed as high as the roof-tops.

'I would only live in this place if I was shipwrecked,' said Josie, picking her way around the cobbles.

'So what now, Batman?' I asked.

'We . . . e . . . ell,' he replied, rubbing his chin thoughtfully, 'I think first we find a bar. Then we find a taxi. Then we find our way back. Agreed?'

'Agreed!' came the triple response.

A few minutes took us into the square, where the only sign of life was a youth tinkering with a moped. Derek, who has a fair knowledge of Spanish, approached him. When he was barely yards away, the lad leapt into the saddle, kick-started and roared off.

'You know, all we want,' mused Joan perceptively, 'is a distant train and Gary Cooper and we've got the plot of a really good western.'

The square was relatively large and as we walked around it, we glanced down various side-streets. They were lined with identical drab cottages, all shuttered and silent. The exception was a recessed, partially opened door, where a witch-type woman hovered in and out of the shadows. Undaunted, Derek made another approach. This time the door was shut, almost in his face, to the accompaniment of sliding bolts. Meanwhile, the temperature soared.

In the corner of the square stood a single-storey shack beneath a Coca Cola sign, and, surprise, surprise, the door was open. We approached cautiously and peered inside the extremely dark interior. As our eyes became accustomed to the gloom, we could see a counter facing us and a floor littered with paper serviettes and fish skeletons. Other than a few bar stools, the only furniture was a formica table, four chairs and a pin-table in the corner of the room. Suddenly a short fat man appeared through a beaded curtain behind the bar. Then, just as quickly, he disappeared again.

'Let's call his bluff and sit down,' whispered Derek.

Throughout our meanderings around the village, the moped rider had followed at a discreet distance. As we sat down, he took up a position astride his now silent machine in the centre of the square. The beaded curtain rattled once more, and we looked up to see a fat man pushing a pretty but reluctant young girl along in front of him. She spoke nervously to Derek in her own tongue.

'Three beers and one lemonade,' he said, in a Spanish that even I could understand.

The fat man then bowed low as the girl scuttled away. She reappeared very soon, however, clutching the ordered four bottles, and placed them hastily on the table. Our host then promptly rushed around the table and picked up each bottle and scolded the girl for not serving the drinks in glasses. 'What will our foreign guests think of us?' translated Derek. With his three-day growth, collar-less shirt and high aroma, 'Not a lot' we could well have said.

The beer was cold and pleasant and, with the exception of Joan's, our glasses were soon empty. There had been much discussion from behind the beaded curtain and suddenly the girl reappeared clutching a table-cloth and a dubious-looking plate of 'nibbles'.

'As they have gone to all this trouble, the least we can do is order another beer,' said Josie encouragingly.

Three more beers were ordered from the now-relaxed girl and a call from Derek summoned the bar owner once more. He sadly declined the offer of a drink, saying he had a funeral to attend. Derek expressed his sympathy and the man bowed yet again and vanished through the beads.

We had all but drained our second beer when the clicking curtain announced the return of our somewhat transformed host. Now shaven (although not washed), he sported a celluloid collar and a black beret. Flashing a broken-toothed smile, he invited Derek to photograph him outside with 'the ladies'. Seeing this as something of a reprieve, in their absence I swept up the fly-blown nibbles into a serviette which I stuffed quickly into Josie's handbag. The photographic party eventually returned and we were all soon joined by a tall middle-aged man who looked rather ill at ease. Derek told us that the newcomer had spent several years in London and allegedly spoke excellent English. The fat man enthusiastically introduced him, then promptly sat back nodding expectantly.

It took just two faltering minutes to realize the man's entire vocabulary consisted of hullo, goodbye, yes, no, and thank you. He looked so wretched that Derek assured the fat man that the newcomer's English was indeed impeccable. Our host celebrated this confirmation by spotting the now-empty plate on the table and swiftly replaced the missing nibbles with an equally nauseous pile and another three beers.

Our presence had by that time drawn the attention of several children. One boy, aged about twelve and braver than most, slowly sidled into the café. He stood staring at us for a while before transferring his attention to the dead pin-ball machine, where he pulled wistfully on the controls.

'Ah, love him,' said Josie maternally and opened her handbag to rummage for some coins.

Obviously puzzled at the sight of the serviette, she tugged it with a shaking motion and spilled the entire contents loose into the deep folds of her bag. The young waitress then pointed to a long lead curled up at the rear of the machine. She indicated that its power was usually taken from the socket at the end of a much-frayed flex. She handed both plug and socket to Derek and placed her hands over her ears. The crackle and resultant sparks were certainly a little disconcerting but the machine lit up well enough and Angelo, as we found his name to be, enjoyed a few games in front of his now braver school friends.

With maternity still very much to the fore, Josie ordered a Coca Cola for the lad. The fat man quickly opened the bottle, but the occasion proved too much for Angelo, who suddenly ran out of the door followed by his friends. The fat man then took off in hot pursuit and returned within minutes with a little rotund five-year-old sweetie, who had obviously been the only one he could catch. He then ordered the child to drink and then gabbled swiftly away to Derek, apparently apologizing for the ingratitude of children.

Meanwhile, the little girl had eye-poppingly drunk the Coke without so much as a pause for breath. When she finished, she slid from the stool and again ran off. Once more the fat man pursued her. Once more he brought her back – this time to thank us for the drink!

All the time this scene was being played, I was aware of the moped-riding youth who sat astride his machine in the square. His curiosity having obtained the better of him, he entered the bar. He circuited our table like a zombie, his eyes never once leaving us. He ordered a beer but was so inattentive to the task of drinking it that he spilt much of it down his shirt. Finally, having satisfied his curiosity, he resumed his vigil from the seat of his moped.

Derek, in asking for a taxi, discovered the bar-owner had a better reason than most for attending the funeral. He was also the 'Dueno de Funeraria' – or undertaker! He was, of course, the village cabbie as well but in this instance, the dead took precedence over the living. However, if we wished to hang around for a while . . . ? Derek thanked him for the gesture but declined the offer. The fat man then shrugged and thanked us profusely for our patronage. Having realized we were not prepared to wait, he conceded there was indeed a second taxi driver in the village. He then directed us somewhat ruefully, to a similar establishment to his own, some half a mile distant.

We were preceded on this walk by the moped rider, who called to the people in each re-opening bar to come and look at the rich foreigners who came and went in taxis, distributed Cokes and gave free sessions on pin-table machines. Just to make it really friendly, in addition to our pathfinder in front we had Angelo and his gang at the rear. Conspicuous by her absence, however, was our Coke-guzzling five-year-old.

'Oh, I do hope she's not exploded,' said Joan worriedly.

We soon saw the bar, and a rusty old Fiat stood patiently outside the front door.

'I think it'll be better if you go in on your own, Derek,' suggested Josie. 'Just tell him we need a cab. I don't think we need go through all the rest of it again, do you? After all, I've already got one bagful of nibbles.'

Judging by the beaming smile of the driver, I should think the twenty-mile trip back to our hotel was probably the best fare he had had in years. Even then there was the additional trip for Derek and Josie on to their hotel.

'Pity you're going back tomorrow,' said Joan as we made our goodbyes. 'I'm sure you would have enjoyed seeing Trish and Gal.'

'Never mind about seeing Trish and Gal,' cut in Derek. 'I'll tell you what we didn't see – we didn't see the bloody flat!'

At exactly eight o'clock on Tuesday morning we were sitting in our hotel foyer, waiting for the coach that was to pick up the intrepid travellers from a selection of hotels in the Marbella area. It was unusually punctual and a smiling girl courier took our tickets as we stepped aboard. The coach was by no means full, and Joan and I decided to spread ourselves over the rear seats. I was mildly surprised that the driver did not accelerate instantly away. Just one foot on the step is usually enough for most Spanish coach drivers. This one had allowed us to reach the sanctuary of the rear seats in unheard-of serenity. I assumed he had had a death in the family. As I looked up to thank him and wave him graciously on our way, I noticed the courier smiling her way towards us.

'Where are your friends?' she beamed. 'We have very little time before the ferry.'

Joan's penny dropped first. 'Our friends . . . Oh no!'

We both knew instantly. We did not need to look back to see who was running out of the hotel foyer. We could close our eyes, though sadly not our ears. There came the patter of four pairs of trainers on the steps, followed by the dreaded cry, 'Oh look Shal, it's Auntie Joan and Uncle Harry. Say hullo to them, they're coming to Tangier with us. Ain't that nice?'

Three to four hours later, we docked at Tangier waterfront. Before disembarking, we were introduced to our guide, who would be with us for the duration of our stay. He was a wispy-bearded, rat-faced little man who, our smiling girl assured us, was undoubtedly the best in Tangier: he answered to the name of 'Raffles'. Best in Tangier he could have been. Raffles he was not. His first action was to count us twice, slowly. He then listed our names.

'Very bad men in Tangier,' he explained. 'But all great respectable of Raffles. You are now Raffles' friends, so you also respectable . . . and safe,' he prudently added.

Our party now consisted of twenty-eight people. Apart from Joan and me and our four nieces and nephews, the rest were couples. These included two white-haired old ladies from Guildford. I cannot remember having a holiday where I did not meet two white-haired ladies from Guildford. Of course, they occasionally claim they live elsewhere. Sometimes it is Bath, sometimes it is Harrogate, but mainly it is Guildford. I once met a Californian who said he firmly believed that no party of twenty or more tourists was allowed to leave England without a statutory pair of white-haired, female septuagenarians. He said he thought we kept them in a shed at Heathrow, where a couple of old dears would be allocated to each departing flight.

'Have you looked out of the porthole?' asked Joan anxiously. 'The quayside is full of people.'

Others had also seen the multitude. 'Why so many people, Raffles?' asked one.

'Much friendly Tangier people, to welcome their guests,' he explained, dubiously.

'Friendly' turned out to be something of an understatement. 'Downright familiar' would have been a more appropriate term. Within minutes of disembarking, I had the feeling the entire population of North Africa had been summoned to greet us. I am now firmly convinced that close on four million Arabs welcome every tourist-laden ferry that plies the Straits of Gibraltar, and their prime function is to rob you blind. I eased my way nonchalantly down the gangplank and into the throng. With my Hong Kong trainers, Marks and Spencer tracksuit and ten-quid instamatic slung affluently around my neck, I had a feeling that the entire Berber nation assumed I was on a secret philanthropic mission on behalf of the Sultan of Oman.

One by one we fought our way on to our coach that was parked on the road that led up from the harbour. An extremely convenient distance, I might add, for the 'Much friendly Tangier people, to welcome their guests.' I was amongst the first to board and Joan soon slipped breathlessly in beside me.

'Well, that was an experience,' she panted. 'I think I managed to keep hold of most things.' She rummaged through her bag. 'Blast! It's gone!'

'Your purse?' I asked worriedly.

'My boiled sweets!' she replied angrily. 'The whole tin has gone.'

I buried my head in my hands in mock disappointment. 'Oh, no! Not your boiled sweets! Tell me it's not your boiled sweets! There I was, thinking we might safari down to Cape Town and now you've blown it by losing your boiled sweets.'

'What have you lost, Auntie Joan?' asked a familiar male voice from four seats away.

'Sadly, not you,' whispered Joan through clenched teeth. 'Oh . . . only some sweets,' she faltered. 'How about you four? Everything intact?'

'We're okay except for Trish. She had some mixed fortune.'

'Mixed?'

'Yeh. Someone nicked her gold name-tag, but on the other hand she got touched up a few times. They do like big girls, these Arabs, you know.'

Well I for one was not going to blame them for that, and as far as I could see, from the contented look on Trish's face, neither was she.

As the last of our party struggled aboard, there was a hydraulic hiss as the door closed. Raffles picked up the coach hand-microphone and cleared his throat.

'Friendly welcome, yes?' (The loud chorus of 'No' did nothing to deter him.) 'Now pay please attention. We go straight to hotel. One hour later, leave again. We go to Casbah. Very dangerous, Casbah. Stay with Raffles all times. Because dangerous, we have extra guide. Very good guide. After Raffles, best guide in Tangier. His name Tangerine. He is my brother-in-law.'

'Did he say Tangerine?' asked Joan incredulously.

'He did indeed,' I assured her.

'Well, what with Shals, Gals, Trishes, Leeses, and Raffles, I'm beginning to think "Joan" is really quite boring. I can hardly wait to see him.'

The coach had just begun to gather speed when an observant member of our party called urgently from the rear seats. 'How about the two old ladies?'

At first, Raffles appeared not to have heard. It was left to some members of the group to try to attract the attention of our smiling girl courier. The fact that she was deep into some mammoth paperback novel had still failed to remove the fixed smile from her face. Others, perhaps with more sense of urgency, yelled at the driver. That gentleman then showed that whatever he was, it was not a linguist. 'STOP! HALTEN! NIX-GO!' all had no effect. However, a particularly loud 'OY!!' caused him to brake as if Mohammed had stepped under the wheels. I made a mental note to discover what 'OY!' meant in Moroccan. There was a quick babble of conversation between driver and guide. This culminated in our driver angrily slamming his engine into reverse and roaring back the two hundred yards to the quayside, amongst a cacophony of protesting car-horns.

The coach door hissed open and Raffles, muttering furiously, strode across to a market trestle, where our two septuagenarians appeared to be haggling with a particularly sinister-looking stallholder over the cost of two fezes. (Or whatever the plural is for fez.) I fully expected him to seize them by their ears and lead them back. I was a little disappointed when this failed to happen.

'See now need for punctuality,' admonished our guide. 'Please in future, always be punctuality. And not . . . not . . . not for *any* reasons, buy from people unless Raffles say yes. Tangier many crooks. Many many crooks.'

We each hung our heads in a sort of communal atonement. Even the hiss of the closing hydraulic door appeared an admonishment.

The hotel was situated in a seedy part of town, with rubbish in the streets and beggars on the pavements. It was a small oppressive building; although good on comfort, it seemed lacking in genuine warmth. An air of sullenness prevailed. The huge Nubian who guarded the door looked as if he had never smiled in his life.

'Remember. One hour only. Do not be late. Raffles and Tangerine will wait.'

Fifty-five minutes later, everyone except the two old

ladies sat to attention on the coach as we dutifully waited for the reappearance of our guide and his new assistant. Our chastisement appeared to have improved the punctuality of everyone, except the very pair it was aimed at. However, even they finally arrived on time. Not a minute early, mind you, but on time nevertheless. A side door of the hotel opened and Raffles stepped out. A pace or so behind him was, unmistakably, Tangerine. He was not dissimilar in facial appearance to Raffles, but there the similarity ended. He was shorter but much broader and, as opposed to Raffles' European suit, he wore a fez and a wide orange and white striped nightshirt. This gave him the appearance of a rather chunky deck-chair. In addition to this he carried a large, furled, orange umbrella.

'This is Tangerine,' announced our guide, reverently.

'As if he could be anyone else,' muttered an anonymous voice somewhere behind.

'Tangerine know everyone and thing in Casbah. At risk of your lives, do not lose sight of Tangerine while in Casbah.'

'Impossible,' said the same voice. 'You couldn't lose sight of him four miles into a dark tunnel.'

Tangerine bowed majestically, first to the left side of the coach, then to the right. 'S'very nice . . . s'very nice.' Then, nodding to the driver he took his seat. The door hissed and we were at last on our way to the sinister Casbah!

We drove for some thirty minutes and, I would estimate, some ten to twelve miles, before rolling to a halt beside a long wall. Tangerine gestured, indicating that we should alight from the coach. Once outside, Raffles formed us into a tight formation.

'S'very nice,' observed Tangerine as he nodded

approval. He then unfurled his bright orange brolly, and as the mid-afternoon sun baked straight down from a cloudless sky, held it high above him.

'Remember,' said Raffles sternly. 'Deal only with traders Tangerine says and above all . . . stay close.'

We all nodded wisely and bunched a little closer. We British are far too wise to be caught by a few grubby traders. Our Victorian blood taught us how to handle these foreigners instinctively – bargain hard but fairly. They respect you for it, you know.

The streets of the Casbah were little more than alleys. The shops varied from compact, well-stocked and well-staffed, to practically holes in the wall, with just one person in attendance. Yet all had one thing in common. They all appeared intimidating, but all seemed cowed by the presence of Tangerine. How lucky we were! The routine was usually the same. A member of our party would pick something they liked, be it a carving, leather skirt or jewellery. Tangerine would go into a huddled conference and a short time later, Raffles would announce the terms were now excellent. Tangerine would smile, nod and point out that the whole deal was 'S'very nice'. Occasionally, small hungry-looking trios of dagger-belted cut-throats would hover menacingly around the fringe of our group. But a few black oaths through his full black beard would cause their immediate retreat.

Whilst in a jeweller's, Trish approached Raffles and told him she was interested in a replacement for her TRICIA necklace. As she bent over the counter to study a few trays of samples, I saw her thin stretch-trousers tighten and Tangerine's eyes light up. Her fortunes, it seemed, were to be 'mixed' once more. 'S'very nice,' he smiled. 'S'very, s'very nice.'

Whether it was the excitement of discovering a gold tag she liked, or a direct result of Tangerine's fingers between her lower buttocks, I cannot say, but she suddenly squeaked and stood up on her toes. With hindsight, I now suspect this may have been a double coup. A bartering huddle then took place and Trish rose on her toes on at least three more occasions before Raffles announced the final result. The jeweller, it appeared, was an old and trusted friend and would therefore actually make a name tag for her! Of course, this would take a little time but as we were scheduled into a restaurant for tea, if we were prepared to call back in a couple of hours Trish could have her TRICIA for the very special price of 7000 pesetas.

'How about that?' enthused Gal. 'You wouldn't get that sort of service back home, would you?'

I experienced a niggling doubt about that particular observation. I had no idea what Gal did for a living, but if he was out of the house for anything over forty minutes a day, I considered it likely that Trish would be receiving *exactly* that sort of service. In fact, she looked the sort of lady who would be spending a great deal of time on her toes.

After a while, we slotted into a rather smooth routine, with each member of the party taking responsibility for at least one compatriot. This way no one was left behind as we meandered on through the Casbah. Perhaps this was not quite true. The two old ladies, with fezes at a jaunty angle, usually managed to be left behind somewhere.

Because we were so well shepherded, I had taken little interest in our direction. I was therefore rather surprised to find our group back at the gate where we had earlier left our coach.

'To restaurant for tea,' called Raffles.

'S'very nice,' assured Tangerine, lowering his umbrella.

The restaurant was just a short journey and everyone, except Joan, passed a few minutes watching the performance of a snake-charmer in the precinct of the building. It was the same one who had originally caught my eye on the poster. Inside, the restaurant proved a stale, musty place but proudly featured four old Arabs seated in a semi-circle, playing *In A Persian Market* on medieval instruments. On the space in front of them, reminiscent of the snake-charmer's cobra, a fourteen-stone belly-dancer wobbled each curve at an alarming speed.

'S'very nice,' came the exclamation. This time not from Tangerine, but from an appreciative Scotsman who obviously had an eye for a whole lot of woman going in many different directions at the same time.

'Ye get too near tae her,' said his wife acidly, 'an' she'll be boxing yer ears wi' her boobs, ye old fool.'

I thought I would like to have seen that.

Our tea was instantly forgettable, and in the absence of old Jock sustaining an aural battering, I was quite happy to hear Raffles order everyone back on the coach. We were sitting comfortably when someone remembered they had not seen the two old ladies since we had left the snake-charmer. I was seized with a terrible fear. What if that cobra was a python? It was certainly a big snake and I had once read that pythons can swallow quite large sheep whole. Well, they certainly were two *little* old ladies, even if they were wearing fezes.

Suddenly our fears were eased. The missing duo appeared around the corner carrying the largest pouffe I have ever seen.

'Real leather,' they chorused in unison.

'S'no good!' hissed Tangerine, with a startling change of vocabulary. The pair were not put off, however, and settled themselves on the back seat and counted their purchases. We set off rather quickly and soon stopped at the now familiar gate of the Casbah.

'All wait on coach,' ordered Raffles. 'Just lady and gentleman who ordered gold tag.'

In the event, Gal, Shal, Trish and Leese all toddled off excitedly through the cobbled entrance. The rest of us were content to wait. Within minutes they reappeared and were soon flaunting the made-to-measure name-tag at anyone who was not quick enough to look away – and even some who were.

'Go and show it to Uncle Harry, Trish. I'm sure he'd love to see it.' I was a bit uppity about that invitation, especially as I had been staring pointedly out of the window since their return.

Raffles stood up and once more cleared his throat. 'Ahem. Ladies and gentlemen. You have just lived safely through the most dangerous part of Africa. Tangerine has got for you many bargains. He has chased off the robbers. He has made sure you were not swindled. Many bad people in Tangier, many bad people. Perhaps . . .' He held out a dirty linen bag; '. . . perhaps you care to show appreciation?'

Murmurs of agreement passed around the coach. There was an immediate rustle of notes and Tangerine bowed magnificently.

The next forty-five minutes were spent negotiating the steep narrow roads of Tangier and we were soon deposited outside the Caliph Hotel. Before we could alight Raffles was once more on his feet.

'As you have seen, driving coach six miles through this city veery deeficult. Beeg maze . . . veery skilful driver.'

Again a linen bag was shaken.

The driver, who had up to this moment been a mute dumpling, swathed in what appeared to be a laying-out shroud, turned beaming and faced the party. He showed four gold teeth and in perfect English said, 'Heath out.'

Raffles gave him an encouraging clap. 'Only English he knows. Learned from dockers many years ago.'

Raffles then made a short speech in which he prayed for our return to his city, happening to mention in passing just what an excellent guide he had been told he was – many times. He also casually let slip that the rate of pay for excellent guides in Tangier was only half what it should be. This made making ends meet particularly difficult: especially with an infirm widowed mother, a leprosy-stricken brother, four young relatives recently orphaned, all living in a shanty-town shack that was soon to be demolished to build a tourist hotel. He prayed for us once again and then took up an obvious position at the foot of the coach steps. There, with great exaggeration, he assisted every one of us individually down the four steps.

We alighted from the coach into the usual hordes of Arabs all offering their eternal bargains. We looked down at them with disdain. Didn't they know? We had been to the Casbah where, with the assistance of our two Moroccan friends, we had secured some *real* bargains. Only our two old ladies stopped to make yet more purchases, but we were all too tired to reproach them. Our hotel room was on the sixth floor and there were several guests waiting for the lift, which carried only four people at a time.

'Would'na wait if I were ye, mate,' advised the Scots

belly-dance fan. 'It's a typical Tangierian lift . . . it does na' work verra well, or verra long.'

We took his advice and walked up to our room. It had been a long day so we decided to give the night-club a miss and, after a leisurely dinner, had a comparatively early night.

We breakfasted early and found we had a couple of hours before the coach was due for our return journey. We decided to grit our teeth and push through the usual crowds of spivs and beggars outside the hotel, and daringly see what else Tangier had to offer the pedestrian tourist. We had been walking for less than five minutes when Joan pointed to an intriguing flight of steps that led up to a rather tatty gate, situated in an even tattier wall. Many local people were toing and froing. 'Let's see what's up there, shall we?'

As we climbed the steps, the buildings beyond the gate looked vaguely familiar. The first shop we came to was definitely familiar – we had been in it the previous afternoon! In fact we had not only been in it but I had purchased a real leather wallet for the specially reduced price of 200 pesetas, negotiated skilfully by Tangerine.

'How much for the wallets?' I said to the proprietor, in the slow deliberate way that all foreign shopkeepers are born to understand.

'One hunder-ed and feefty pesetas, sir.'

'A hundred and fifty!' I exclaimed.

'Okay, okay, sir. Because of nice lady, I give you special price . . . one hunder-ed pesetas.'

Joan and I stared incredulously at each other. 'Tanger-bloody-ine!' we exploded simultaneously.

How about that hair-raising coach ride we had just walked in five minutes, door-to-door? Where were all the sinister-looking cut-throats? The Casbah suddenly appeared about as sinister as Sainsbury's. We began to make the rounds of the shops we had entered the previous afternoon. The story was the same. Every shopkeeper spoke almost perfect English and asked one third of the price.

Joan snapped her fingers. 'The jeweller's! Let's find the jeweller's!'

'What bloody jeweller's?'

'The jeweller's where that Trish ordered her name-tag necklace, of course.'

'Oh . . .' I shook my head in mock disapproval. 'You've got a nasty mind you have . . . come on then . . . quick!'

We found the shop with surprising ease – but then we had found everything else with ease that morning.

'Could we see some gold name-tags, please?' Joan asked.

'Ceertainly, madam. Engleesh name?'

'Of course.' She said it as if there were only English names in the whole world. 'What names do you have?'

'I have *all* names, madam. Here . . .' He pulled two drawers from beneath the counter. The items were not even neatly displayed. They were simply two large, individual heaps. There must have easily been a hundred in each drawer. 'All same price, madam. 4500 pesetas. But because I like English ladies . . .' he threw both hands in the air in a carefree gesture '. . . 3900 pesetas.'

'How about an . . . er . . . difficult name? Is it more expensive?'

'Deeficult?' He shrugged. 'No proobleem. We feex it here.' He pointed to a bead curtain at the rear of the shop. 'All name-tags same price.'

Whilst this conversation was taking place, I was preparing to run. There was no doubt at all that this lad was expecting a sale. He was not going to be best pleased when he discovered it was morbid curiosity. I could already feel the embarrassment creeping up on me. Joan, on the other hand, can be quite clinical in a shop. She can say, 'No it's not what I want,' and leave, whereas I will buy any crap imaginable just to get out. Years of experience have taught me exactly when that moment comes. I already had one foot out of the door when she began the first word. 'No,' she said curtly. Halfway through the sentence, I had removed *both* feet from the premises. By the time she had reached the word 'want' I was practically out of the Casbah.

It was now time to hurry back to the hotel for our coach for the ferry. One look at the faces told us we were not the only ones who had walked six miles in three minutes. Never mind, with any luck Raffles would be with us at least to the ferry. Those of us who had bought letter-openers in the form of Arabic daggers were quite looking forward to the confrontation. Our anticipation was shattered by our smiling English courier.

'I'm afraid it is time we were all on the coach,' she announced.

'Where's Raffles?' we pleaded.

'I'm afraid he left on the night ferry. He has some urgent business in Spain this afternoon.'

'He'd have had some urgent business in Tangier this morning,' cried a frustrated voice from the back of the foyer, 'if I could have laid hands on him.'

There was a rattle as at least six of us thrust our letter-openers back in their scabbards.

As the coach pulled away from the hotel front, I suddenly realized that the pavement was clear for the first time since our arrival. It was as if the word had been passed – the tree has been picked clean, there is no more to be had.

'Well, at least we did all right, Trish,' sang out Gal in a voice just loud enough to invite a rejoinder. 'A made-to-measure necklace at that price has still got to be a bargain.'

'A bargain is it?' sniffed the Scotsman. 'Dinna delude ye'self mate. The only bargain ye'll git in this place, is ta sell yer missus ta the sheik.'

I may have imagined it, but for a moment I could have sworn I saw a look of interest pass over the buxom Trish's face.

'Are you going to tell her?' I whispered to Joan.

'Tell who what?' she replied.

'Tell Trish about the jeweller's, of course.'

'No, I feel sorry enough for her as it is, putting up with that twit all the time. Let her keep thinking she has a bargain. She'll realize soon enough once her neck goes green.'

'Why is her neck going green?'

'Because there is more gold in your trouser-zip than in a dozen of those "real gold" necklaces.'

I put on an instant superior look. 'So I've been told . . . many times,' I added casually.

'Well, you just be careful,' she warned. 'Green can be a very worrying colour.'

We had barely reached the corner of the street when I realized that we were yet again minus our two septuagenarians. 'Oy!' I yelled to the driver. Once more he stopped on a sixpence.

'You really *must* find out what "Oy" is in Moroccan,' mused Joan.

'Why the panic?' smiled our courier.

'The two old dears, they're missing again,' I explained.

'No, they are not,' she said. 'They're staying on. They like it so much here that they have booked for another week. They are returning on next Wednesday's ferry.'

Two hours later, as our ferry throbbed its way across the straits, Joan and I leaned against the guardrail and watched Tangier ease slowly into the horizon. I had just thrown my last souvenir of the place into the sea. It was, appropriately, a bad orange.

'Well, I think that's cured me of Africa,' said Joan.

I eased in closer to her. 'Listen,' I whispered confidentially. 'When we get back to Marbella, there is an excursion that leaves on Thursday morning for Cadiz. How does it grab you? I've spoken to Trish and Gal and they are very keen indeed . . .'

Confessions of a Condiment Smuggler

'Listen, Aitch, twenty-two of us from the nick have decided to go on holiday to Florida for a couple of weeks. I thought it would be a nice gesture to you and Joan to ask you both along. You never know, it might start a take-a-pensioner-on-holiday scheme.'

'Well, Martin! That's really nice of you! I am really quite touched. It's nice to know that even though I'm retired, I am not forgotten. Whether we come or not, I would like you to thank the rest of the group for their kind thoughts. It means a lot to me, I can tell you.'

'Er, well,' he faltered. 'I wouldn't say anything to them at the moment if I was you. You see, they think John and Jean Rivers are coming but Jean's just discovered she's pregnant and they can't now afford it.'

'Oh I see!' I replied, my tone changing. 'I've been taken from the subs' bench, have I? I was never in the first team at all. In fact, if it wasn't for the coming little River I wouldn't rate a mention?'

'Now, now, Aitch, that's not so,' he protested. 'I mean, you would have been amongst the first I would have considered normally. It's just that . . . well . . . you being a pensioner and everything – '

'I couldn't stand the pace, eh?'

'Well, we do have one or two *young* ones in the group, you know.'

'Martin,' I said, in what I hoped was my icy tone. 'I assume we won't be walking there, will we? It will be a proper aeroplane and everything?'

'Of course.'

'Then when we arrive there, there will be beds, electric lights and running water?'

'Aitch . . . Aitch . . . AITCH!' he sang out, his voice increasing with every syllable. 'You are going well over the top, you know.' He gave a deep sigh. 'All I want to know is, one, are you coming? And two, don't say anything until I've had a chance to mentally prepare the rest of the party.'

'Thanks, Martin. That's made me feel really great.'

'I'm pleased about that, Aitch. I'll phone you again next week with the details. Cheers.'

The truth was, although I would never have admitted it to him, I was absolutely delighted with Martin's offer. Joan and I had been discussing making that very trip. I had even reached the stage where I had collected a couple of fly-drive brochures. Then out of the blue came his telephone call.

Six days later, having, I assume, broken the news to the rest of the party, Martin telephoned once more with full details. We were to be a group of twenty-four, nine couples and six WPCs. We were booked at a Fort Lauderdale motel to start with. Then, after a few nights, we were to drive across the state to Clearwater, to stay a few days there before moving on to Orlando to take in Disneyland. Two hundred miles down the turnpike would bring us back for our final night in Miami before our flight home. In addition to planning our route, he had arranged for the hiring of six cars, the collection of our visas, a coach to pick us up to and from our homes to Gatwick airport and, for good measure, had also thrown in a little sound financial advice. Martin, in short, was not just a gem but an organizing wonder.

'I don't believe it,' said Joan, as we waited that chill May morning at the corner of our street for the coach to arrive. 'You say he has arranged *everything* himself?'

'Uh-huh.'

'But no man is that competent – especially a policeman. There's a trap here somewhere, I know it.'

'Hasn't everything been correct so far?' I asked smugly.

'Yes – and it's that which is worrying me. I'm not used to it.'

At 9.59 a.m., the coach, which Martin had said would arrive 'somewhere about ten o'clock' glided smoothly into sight. As it rolled to a standstill in front of us, the door hissed open. The sound of the coach radio could clearly be heard – the pips for the ten o'clock news.

'Martin,' called Joan as she climbed the four steps, 'would you care to accompany us on *every* holiday? Or at the very least, make our arrangements?'

'Thanks,' smiled our benefactor as he checked his list. 'That's the tenth offer I've had this morning . . . anyway, you're the last, so roll 'em, driver. It's westward ho for the constabulary!'

As I looked around the coach, I was delighted by whom I saw. I not only knew and had worked with everyone present, but would have been hard pushed to have wished for a better bunch. This had certainly been an aspect that had bothered me. Two weeks with *any* workmate could be at best 'iffy' and at worst, murderous. The only remaining question was, with whom would we share the car?

Martin, with his customary aplomb, read my mind.

'Aitch, you and Joan share with Keith and Ann; suit you?'

'Suits us fine, mate. Suits us fine.'

Joan tugged my sleeve. 'But how do Keith and Ann feel about it?' she whispered.

It had simply never occurred to me they would be other than delighted. 'They'll be as pleased as Punch, of course.'

'Yes . . .' she sighed, with the merest shake of her head, '. . . I just thought you might say that.'

The car-hire complex at Miami airport is very close to international arrivals, which is just as well because the southern tip of the Sunshine State was having its first downpour in months. It was dark, wet and unbelievably humid. The twenty-four of us huddled in the office as a huge clerk allocated our cars. Ours was the last of the six, and with bent heads the four of us struggled with our cases to the furthest corner of the yard.

'Don't forget what Martin said,' Ann reminded Keith. 'Make sure of the route and on no account go into downtown Miami at night.'

'Then don't let the others out of your sight,' replied Keith curtly. 'I don't know the way and the only map we have is for Disneyland.'

'If it's got a Big Bad Wolf on it then I'm treating it as an omen,' said Joan prophetically.

'Don't you *really* know the way, Keith?' asked Ann, with just a hint of nervousness.

'Not to worry,' he chirped, as he threw their two cases into the car boot. 'As long as we keep the others in sight we'll be fine.'

We settled into the car, Keith and I in front, where we were to take it in turns to drive, and the ladies in the rear. He spent a few moments familiarizing himself with the lay-out. First the wipers clicked, then the lights flashed, and finally the horn blew. I would have been more confident if I had not suspected he had been looking for the trafficators. Still, two out of three wasn't bad.

'They are beginning to leave, Keith,' said Ann, pointing anxiously at the line of rear lights moving slowly through the complex gates.

'So are we love, don't worry.'

He turned the key a fraction more and the engine roared willingly into life. He fiddled for a second to find reverse. Succeeding, he looked over his shoulder for vision. Yet the instant he did so he stopped, and put the engine back into neutral. He then turned once more and came face-to-face with his wife.

'Ann,' he said curtly, 'where are my glasses?'

'You've got them on,' she pointed out.

I began to experience a certain disquiet. I had known this lad for years; surely he knew if he was wearing his specs or not?

'Not *these* glasses,' he said slowly. '*These* glasses are my *reading* glasses. What I want are my *driving* glasses.'

This was the first time Joan and I had experienced the dozen-times-daily ritual of the wrong glasses. It was to become quite a feature of the next two weeks. As far as I could understand, Keith had two pairs of glasses. (At least, he assured me he had two pairs.) These were reading glasses and driving glasses. Again as far as I could make out, whenever he had to read anything, he would be wearing his driving glasses. Conversely, whenever he had to drive, he would be wearing his reading glasses. Considering he had but *two* pairs, I could never understand how he could consistently be in possession of the wrong pair. On the law of averages alone he should have been okay for at least fifty per cent of the time. But no! Not once! Not once in two weeks and fifteen hundred miles did that man have the correct glasses.

But the mystery did not end there. For on every one of the hundred occasions when he discovered he had the wrong glasses, he would always look accusingly at his wife. The phrase 'Ann! Where are my glasses?' became such a feature of the dialogue in our car, that if we had bought a mynah bird, the thing would have said nothing else. Having said that, I must also say that to spend two weeks with that pair was an absolute joy. I don't think Joan stopped laughing.

By now, the confusion in the car park was causing us all some concern. Bags were unzipped, pockets turned out and all the time those guiding rear lights were slipping further and further away. Suddenly the obvious answer to our problem struck me. *I* would drive – I don't need glasses for driving. It was at this moment that the elusive specs appeared, and with a quick flurry they were in place. I stared hard at these much-sought-after specs. No wonder there was confusion, the damn things appeared identical.

'Why don't you paint one of the buggers red or something,' I demanded. 'You wouldn't have this stupid problem any more.'

Keith was not listening. He now had his specs and was in full control of the car. We screeched around the yard between the rows of parked vehicles and roared towards the gate. The rear lights had certainly disappeared, but with luck we could still catch them. We were only yards from the gate when an alarm bell sounded and a red and white barrier dropped swiftly across our path. For the moment we were not going anywhere.

The giant clerk appeared at the office door. If he looked no bigger than before, he was certainly more intimidating. His hand flashed to his hip.

'He's got a gun!' I yelled. 'Keep still!'

We froze to our seats as his hand swung up to reveal a sinister-looking black *note-book*.

'You've got the wrong car, man,' he drawled, glancing down at the pages.

'But we're with the other cars,' I bleated, pointing to the now-empty road.

'You've got the wrong car, man,' he repeated, just a little slower and a tiny bit more deliberately.

'I think he's saying we've got the wrong car,' whispered Ann, 'and I for one take his point.'

As far as I was ever able to ascertain, the confusion boiled down to a question of colour. We had taken a green and we should have taken a red. Ten minutes later, we roared out of the car park in a red Ford, hopelessly lost on a wet night, with a Mickey Mouse map.

'You'd better pass me that map, Keith,' I suggested. 'I'll see if I can make something of it.'

He eased a crumpled paper sheet from his hip pocket. 'I'll tell you now, I'm not optimistic,' he murmured. 'If you thought a note-book was a revolver, God knows what you'll make of a twenty-four-inch map and a picture of the Three Little Pigs.'

All we knew of our destination was that it was a Best Western Motel in Fort Lauderdale. As to getting there, we had not a clue – the map was of Orlando, 200 miles away. The car-park clerk had hardly been helpful, convinced as he was of our intention to take the wrong vehicle. 'Get to the freeway and ask' was as far as he would commit himself. As to the location of the freeway, or even what a 'freeway' was, we had not a clue. We drove aimlessly for a couple of miles. It was by now quite late, we had not seen one pedestrian and the streets were sleazy and deserted. Suddenly we saw the lights of an all-night gas station.

'I'll go,' I volunteered bravely.

As I slid from the car, the humidity was like walking through warm water. On reaching the office, I realized how fortunate we were to be desiring directions and not petrol. There were two occupants, so drunk they could barely stand. The good thing was they took instantly to my accent and insisted on giving me a free map of Miami; the bad thing was, they also insisted on directing me. I left them on the verge of blows over the advisability of a left or right turn at some suburban intersection and we were once more on our way – only this time with a pigless map.

Fort Lauderdale turned out to be about four times further than I had imagined, although it was also a straight, easy road. Our route took us clear through the centre of town and soon we could clearly see the name of our motel on our left. It was now nearly midnight and we were a good two hours adrift.

'I bet the others have all been worried sick about us,' said Ann guiltily. 'I can just imagine what they'll say, can't you?'

We agreed their relief would be tremendous. Keith stopped the car on the motel forecourt and we soon heard those old familiar voices coming from the direction of the swimming pool. We decided to head there to put their minds at rest before we even checked in at reception.

I remember my first reaction – that for a group so upset, they were disguising it pretty well. There appeared to be a great deal of hilarity, water-splashing and chinking glasses. Not really the cacophony that should emerge from an anxious group of friends beside themselves with worry.

'Yoo hoo!' I called. 'We've arrived at last!'

The nearest to us were the six girls and Duncan. They were sitting around a table with an impressive collection of empty glasses. Duncan was rather surprisingly attired in a natty pair of swim-trunks and a particularly neat, striped tie – but nothing else. Surprising though Duncan's appearance was, I felt I should study the six girls more closely. I was used to seeing them in uniform, but I wanted to be sure I recognized them properly now they were out of it – and out of almost everything else, I was shocked to see.

'Come on, Aitch!' yelled Martin from the pool. 'The water's great. Why haven't you four changed yet?'

'Why haven't we – the buggers haven't missed us!!' exploded Keith. 'Would you believe it! We could have finished up in Cuba for all they knew!'

Joan sidled up to me. 'See,' she said knowingly. 'He's not infallible after all.'

Our room was excellent, with masses of space. As I dumped our cases in an alcove, Joan followed me with our hand-luggage. As she placed the two holdalls on the bed, one slipped and spilt its contents on to the floor. In addition to the usual traveller's junk, I was surprised to see a varied assortment of small packets and sachets.

'Hullo hullo hullo!' I said, in my best constabulary manner. 'How long have we been dealing in cannabis then?'

'Fine copper you must have been if you can't tell cannabis from condiments. Besides, they are nothing to do with you. They're for Jenny. She asked us all to collect them, just before the first meal on the plane . . . you were asleep at the time.'

'Collect them?' I echoed. 'Why does she want packets of salt and pepper, for heaven's sake?'

'It's not just salt and pepper. It's sugar, mustard, powdered milk and face-wipes. You'd be surprised how much you can collect on just one flight. Anyway, nearly half of that is yours.'

'I can *see* what it is,' I pointed out irritably. 'What I want to know is why she *wants* it.'

'It's her mortgage. She's in the process of buying a flat and cash is a bit tight at the moment.'

'So she's selling salt and pepper packets?'

'No, you fool. She simply wants us to collect as many of these things as possible so she can stock her larder when she gets home.'

Jenny was the youngest of our WPCs and at the end of a long, tiring day could look all of sixteen years, instead of her proper age, which I swear was about twelve. She was also the station sweetheart.

'That kid's too young to buy a fiat. She should still be playing with a doll's house.'

'That "kid", as you call her, is a competent, attractive, twenty-two-year-old policewoman, as no doubt you noticed a few minutes ago when you were staring down her bikini.'

'Listen, I'm showing no favouritism on this tour, I'm staring down *everyone's* bikini. There's no point in me coming on holiday with six good-looking young women if I am not going to enjoy it, so for the next two weeks I shall be staring down bikinis and up skirts.'

'Spoken like a true middle-aged man! Now if your poor

old back will allow it, do you think you could pick up those packets and find somewhere safe to store them?'

'But do you realize,' I said, 'that if twenty-four of us are spending the next two weeks collecting condiments, she'll have a ton by the time we get home?'

'Good! That's what we're hoping for. Now that's not much to ask, is it?'

On the face of it, I had to agree. It was not much to ask. At least it would *not* be *much* to ask a normal person but normality flies out of the window once someone sets Joan on one of her collecting missions. Her zeal becomes mindblowing. I remember a neighbour who once asked us to save our old newspapers for the Scouts. After a month he begged us to stop. She had piled so much paper in his porch that he could not get in his front door. Then there were bottle-tops for a guide-dog, clothes for the Salvation Army, stamps, ring-pulls, foreign coins and rags. It was against this background that I was dreading this new venture – condiments, powdered milk and face-wipes!

'Couldn't we pay her mortgage for a month?' I whined. 'It would be a lot less trouble.'

As a party we got on well. Much of this no doubt stemmed from the fact that each car group did their own thing during the day. (Which, in our case, was looking for Keith's glasses.) We would then usually meet up in the evening for a drink and to swop adventures. It was during one of these soirées that three of the girls, Jenny, Melinda and Anne (with an 'e' as opposed to Keith's wife) mentioned they had been chatted up by members of the local police force, who were surprised to discover they were similarly employed. The police must have contacted the local paper, who decided to feature a piece with photographs, its theme being, 'Three-young-WPCs-who-look-like-this-and-carry-no-guns.' This decision may not have been entirely uninfluenced by the photogenic quality of the trio.

The same day the story appeared, we were asked, via the three girls, if we wished to play the local police in a volleyball game next morning on the beach. It seemed a sociable idea and we readily agreed, even though few of us had even seen the game, never mind played it. Our directions were to go to the Sandpiper Hotel on the water's edge where we would meet our hosts. Because the girls had made only provisional arrangements, we were not too sure of the day's programme. How long were we expected to stay? Would it include lunch?

It was a large hotel and as our six cars came to a halt, we expected we would have to ask around before we could find anyone who knew of our hosts. To our surprise, not only were we expected but the red carpet was well and truly out. The manager welcomed us with cocktails and canapés and again the local press appeared. The reporter, and particularly the photographer, were delighted to discover we had another three girls up our sleeves, in the shape of Beverley, Karen and Elaine. With these three lasses, shape was the operative word. Cameras again clicked merrily – but not before the manager had handed round top quality sweatshirts with the hotel's name and crest boldly emblazoned on front and rear.

'It's like being on tour with the "Bluebell Group",' said Keith, changing his specs for the twenty-third time.

It took a while, but it slowly dawned on us that the whole operation was just an excellent publicity feature for the hotel. Anything like it at home would have given the

Commissioner a hernia and caused questions to be asked in the House, yet here in America, no one thought it amiss.

The day was an enormous success, and the typical American generosity of our hosts ensured we had all eaten too much. This whole question of food had begun to be a problem. Although we were eating no more meals than we would at home, the sheer size of them was stultifying.

'I think I am going to cut out breakfast in the mornings,' announced Joan. 'For the rest of this holiday I shall just have coffee and juice.'

We all agreed it was an excellent idea and breakfast-time next morning was to be the start of our self-discipline.

Joan and I arrived first at the breakfast-bar, where every item on the menu was numbered. Orange juice and coffee, for example, was number two. Ham and eggs, number five, and so on. Joan and I both ordered our 'twos' and further down the counter I noticed that Keith and Ann had also arrived. We acknowledged them with a wave, then dawdled over our coffee with a ton-weight American newspaper. Suddenly the waitress hurried by with a tray on which was the largest breakfast I had ever seen.

'Just look at that plate!' exclaimed Joan. 'It's colossal . . . and it's for Keith!'

I could not believe my eyes. It really was an enormous meal. I looked quickly down the menu to see just what my co-driver was going to have to work his way through before we could start the day's adventures. It could have only been the one dish, number fourteen: 'The Florida Husky Breakfast'! This consisted of two of everything plus pancakes and maple syrup. I just had to discover the reason for such a dramatic change of mind. Paying our bill, we hastened down to the end of the counter to where Keith still stared horror-struck at the duos of eggs, hams, grits, tomatoes, mushrooms and sausages. Plus of course, pancakes and maple syrup.

'What on earth possessed you to order that lot?' I asked.

'Well go on,' urged Ann. 'Tell him.' He mumbled something I did not hear. 'Tell him properly,' she insisted.

'I forgot my bloody glasses and couldn't see the menu,' he boomed angrily, 'so I just guessed it.'

'But why didn't you ask someone? Ann, for example.'

She sat with her lips pursed and her gaze fixed firmly on the ceiling. The subject had obviously been raised before and Keith is not a man to whom one airs the same subject twice in under a minute, particularly to his detriment. I still had visions of a friend of ours sitting on the canteen floor with his entire dinner spread over his chest. He had been silly enough to upset Keith. Well, I certainly wasn't going to upset him, not with a Florida Husky Breakfast in front of him I wasn't.

'Er . . . I just hope you enjoy it, son . . . we'll see you in the car.'

'You'll never guess,' said Ann, some forty minutes later. 'He ate every bit. Said it was delicious and he might have it again tomorrow.'

The next morning I watched him. He didn't.

Halfway through our tour found us at Clearwater, a resort on the west coast of Florida. We had, by this time, made our own adjustments to the size of the American meal. We had moved from the extremes of fruit juice and coffee, to say nothing of the solidifying Florida Husky, to a more sensible compromise. This consisted of a small cooked breakfast, scrambled eggs on toast or such like, via lunch-time fruit to a have-what-you-like dinner. The advantage of this idea was that we not only looked forward to the evening meal, but even more importantly, always enjoyed it.

One of the aspects of eating out in America is the standard of service. We became, I suppose, quite boring in our repetitive praise of American restaurants. We delighted both in the service and the quality of the food. Or that is, we did, until we reached Clearwater. On the other hand, I have to say it was different.

We had spent a long day on the beach and, by evening, were really hungry. We had been recommended to a hotel restaurant by two local policemen we had met that afternoon. At least I *think* they were policemen. They *said* they were policemen, and they certainly had the word 'Police' displayed many times on their apparel (I hesitate to say uniform). The four of us had gone to a beach-café for our lunchtime fruit, when the two constables entered. They were dressed in blue trainers, short white socks, blue shorts with white trim, white tee-shirts with blue trim and baseball caps with 'Clearwater Police' inscribed. Hanging from the belt of each was a revolver, radio and handcuffs.

'Something looks out of place,' observed Joan, as the pair settled themselves in front of two massive dishes of multi-coloured ice-cream and fruit.

'I think it's the armoury,' said Keith. 'I don't think it quite goes with the play-suits and the knickerbocker-tropical, sunrise-glory, peach-and-strawberry, fresh-cream sundae.'

'Well,' said Joan sympathetically, 'the temperature is in the nineties. You can't really expect the poor dears to go around in boots and button-up tunics. Besides, in comparison to many American policemen, they look quite friendly.'

'In *that* outfit you *have* to be friendly,' muttered Keith disapprovingly. 'No one can be belligerent in little white socks and a pretty-boy tee-shirt. Least of all a copper.'

The pair seemed intrigued by our attention and we passed an interesting twenty minutes or so with them. It was during this conversation that they recommended the hotel restaurant. 'Best damn place in the county,' was their verdict. So it was at the 'best damn place in the county' that we sat round a table for four just before seven o'clock that evening.

The hotel appeared of medium size and the restaurant was certainly well appointed, with red plush and chandeliers being the order of the day. The room looked as if it could seat around 200 customers but there were only some eighteen to twenty present. However, it was still fairly early. A young, smiling blond waiter approached.

'Mmmm,' murmured Joan appreciatively. 'He's dishy.' His appearance did little for me so I took her word for it.

'Evening folks,' he greeted us warmly, '. . . and just what can I do for you good people?'

Yes, there was no doubt about it, I thought, this was yet another restaurant maintaining the high standard we had come to expect in the States. We had a few pleasant verbal exchanges and he recommended the calves' liver as being particularly worthwhile. Calves' liver it is then, we agreed. Off he went with an order for four plus a carafe of house red and three soups. Off he went – but he did not come *back*. Well, not for twenty minutes he didn't. When he did, it was quite a surprise.

'Evening folks,' he greeted us warmly, '. . . and just what can I do for you good people?'

'I think we've done that bit,' said Keith, not unkindly. 'I believe we are on the calves' liver for four and a carafe of red house-wine bit now.'

'Oh, of course!' laughed the waiter, without a hint of embarrassment. 'My mistake. Calves' liver and red wine it is – right away.'

'And three soups,' I reminded him.

'And three soups most *definitely*, sir.'

The delay this time was almost bearable. Little more than seven or eight minutes.

'Sorry folks,' he smiled, 'liver's off.'

'Off?' echoed Keith, staring pointedly at his watch. 'But it's only 7.30 p.m.'

'I know sir, I know,' he soothed, 'but liver is very popular tonight. If you permit me though, I can also recommend the veal cordon-bleu sir, Most excellent it is.'

'Well, do you think we could have a drink while we wait?' I asked.

'Ah yes, of course sir! Carafe of house red, wasn't it?'

I nodded.

I must admit he was back soon enough. Still smiling, he carried in a carafe on a tray with four frosted glasses. This was something of a surprise because we already had two wine glases each, albeit empty.

'Here you are, sir.' He placed the wine on the table. 'I think you'll find this most enjoyable . . . almost worth the wait, sir.'

'But that's *rosé* surely,' I pointed out.

He glanced quickly down. 'Rosé it is most certainly, sir! D'you think I should kill the barman?'

'If there's to be a choice, I think we'd prefer a suicide pact,' suggested Keith.

By this time he had placed our eight original glasses on to his tray. He then had to move them over to accommodate the returned rosé. Unflurried, he once more left our table on an errand of correction.

'Well who's going to tell him when he comes back?' asked Keith.

'Tell him what?' questioned Joan.

'Tell him he's fetched us four iced glasses for the rosé but we'll need our others back for the red wine.'

He again appeared, but before we could utter a word he cut in first. 'I'm afraid we're fresh out of soup spoons, sir.'

'Can I use my teaspoon?' asked Joan, more in fun than with any serious intention.

'I would if I were you, madam,' he confided. 'You'll find soup lasts very much longer that way.'

'Wait a minute, wait a minute,' I interrupted. 'How many rooms in this hotel . . . two hundred?'

'I'd say that, sir.'

'– And there's twenty people in here tonight?'

'I'd say that too, sir.'

'So how come there's no soup spoons?'

He thought carefully for a moment, tapping his nose thoughtfully with his finger tip. 'I'll walk out, sir, shall I?'

'Not before you've returned our wine glasses you won't!' Keith informed him curtly.

Joan, who is teetotal anyway, was clearly enjoying the whole débâcle. 'Can I ask you a question, young man?'

'Certainly madam, most certainly you can.'

'Is there a cover-charge for your act?'

Yet again the waiter left.

'So far,' said Keith as we waited for our trio of glasses to be returned, 'we've been here for forty minutes, we've spoken to the waiter half a dozen times and all we've managed to do is to order.'

'But he *is* pretty though,' approved Ann.

It may have been predictable, but the meal, when it finally came, turned out to be superb.

'I bet he's the chef as well,' said Joan, her faith in him touching to behold. 'And I'll tell you something else, Keith.' She paused for a second. 'He changes glasses more often than you do!'

On leaving the hotel car park, I was faced with a small difficulty. To drive back to our motel necessitated turning left on to a dual carriageway. No problem really, or at least, it shouldn't be. Yet for some reason, although I quickly became used to driving on the 'wrong' side of the street, I seemed to have a particular blindspot about turning left on to dual roads. Sometimes I would try to turn immediately left, which of course would put me on the wrong side of the road entirely. This was never as alarming as it sounds, because the three instant screams from inside our car always prevented the matter becoming serious. On other occasions, I would cross to the correct side well enough but I would then turn into the *first* lane. In America, of course, this is the fast lane. Within seconds, cars as long as the street would be blasting my eardrums, nudging my bumper and flashing more lights than a son et lumière.

It was with this in mind that I drove out on to the freeway. Don't forget, I told myself, go as far as possible before turning left. Relieved to have remembered my weakness, I then joined in the general discussion on the entertainment value of our waiter. I safely cleared the first half of the road, then, easing through the central reservation, prepared to turn left, at the same time dutifully remembering to miss the fast lane. There was little traffic and I remember being agreeably surprised at what a nice wide road it was. I eased across into the fourth lane and completed my left turn. I then braked to a halt, switched off and buried my head in my hands. In my obsession to avoid turning too soon, I had turned too late. There was not a fourth lane at all. I had driven into the empty car park of the hotel opposite.

'Of course, I realized exactly what you did,' said Keith, almost tutorially. 'But instead of dropping your head when you switched off, if you had said "Shan't be long, just popping out for a piss," I would have been well impressed.'

By the time we reached Orlando, the temperature was consistently in the mid-nineties. Disneyland, as a spectacle, had taken our breath away. Like many Britons, we had suspected it would be little more than a larger version of the Blackpool or Southend funfairs. We never realized it would be a fantasy city in its own right. We had each bought a 'two-day' ticket and after the first day there were still a great number of sights and shows yet to be seen. Sadly, whether it was the heat, or the Clearwater waiter exacting a belated 'own-back', we were not sure, but Keith and Ann developed stomach upsets and stayed at the motel the second day.

Joan and I therefore had the car to ourselves. 'It really was too hot in Disneyland yesterday,' she sighed. 'How about trying somewhere else today?'

'Well, I've heard about Disney Village. They say it's less crowded and less commercial; let's try there.'

So Disney Village it was. It was still hot of course, but as we sat on the grass under the trees by the lakeside, listening to a sixteen-piece band play Glenn Miller music, I came to a serious conclusion.

'You know,' I confided. 'From now on I am going to be good for the rest of my life.'

Joan eyed me suspiciously. 'And what fetched this on?'

'This place,' I announced. 'This place is heaven . . . and I want to come here again when I die.'

'Hmmm,' she responded thoughtfully. 'There's something in that; perhaps I might join you after all.'

'Not if you're still stealing condiments you won't. Glenn Miller don't play for crooks.'

The following day, our six-car convoy rolled down the Florida turnpike, bound for Miami and the last night of our holiday. Keith and Ann were thankfully recovered, even to the extent of being once more embroiled in his endless quest for the correct spectacles. The whole party had decided on a final get-together to celebrate the success of the venture and, more importantly, to thank Martin, our organizer. There was to be nothing grand, just a few drinks around the pool. Even this was not to pass without incident.

Valerie, Duncan's wife, had been a little unlucky with her body surfaces. She was a very fair-complexioned girl and had been badly burnt by the sun on our very first day. It was too late when we discovered that her sole protection against the ninety-degree heat had been a twice-daily smear of Nivea cream. She didn't even use a sun lotion. Whether it was the subsequent lotions and potions she used to soothe her angry flesh, we were not sure, but she suddenly appeared to be the target of every tiny winged insect south of Canada. This gave her an almost neurotic dread of anything with wings or in possession of more than two legs.

By the last few days of the holiday her soreness had vanished, but the peeling and eruptions persisted, and although usually a quite attractive girl, she did have a temporary resemblance to the surface of Mars. Understandably, particularly in the humidity of the late evenings around the poolside, she tended belatedly to err on the side of safety by spending most of her time under cover.

This particular evening, she was washing her hair in the bathroom basin. Duncan had painstakingly cleared, not just every fly and midge, but even odd-shaped dust from the room. The basin was full of foam and the girl had her hair draped down into the suds with her face just an inch or two from the water. Feeling even warmer than usual, she reached blindly for the fan switch which clicked instantly into operation. Even through the humming of the motor and the bubbling of the suds, she thought she heard another noise – a sort of 'plop' noise.

Clearing the suds with her hands, she reached down into clear water and washed the shampoo from her eyes. She then discovered she had most definitely heard a plop. Resting leisurely on the fan, doubtless admiring the view, had been a cockroach the size of a rogue alligator. The first revolution of the blades had thrown him off and straight into the fair Valerie's soap-suds. In her present state, coming literally face-to-face with such a beast must have been akin to being fed to a dragon. They do say her screams could be heard in Bermuda.

The following evening we all assembled in the departure lounge at Miami airport; all, that is, with the exception of Beverley. She had relatives in town and had arranged to join us just before departure. A French air traffic controllers' strike was due in a few hours and an airport announcement told us that in an effort to avoid delays at Gatwick, our flight would leave twenty minutes early. This caused us no little apprehension because Beverley was not aware of this earlier departure, and even though she should have been at the airport in plenty of time, the chances were she would cut it very fine. The first call was made, but aware of her absence, none of us moved. On the third call we could wait no longer and our whole group trooped reluctantly towards the exit. Half had gone through when Jenny exclaimed, 'There she is!'

We gestured frantically to her as she strolled leisurely in at the far end of the hall. Someone had just reached the 'Where-the-hell-have-you-been-because-' stage when Beverley let out a loud 'Eek!' and ran back out of the lounge. At first, we thought it was Valerie's pterodactyl making a comeback, but it proved to be nothing more sinister than her realization that she had omitted to purchase her full quota of duty-frees.

'Just how do these girls make such good policewomen?' asked Joan despairingly. 'I swear half of them are daft.' Being teetotal of course, she does fail to recognize the advantages of a good duty-free. 'On second thoughts,' she added, 'you needn't answer that. Married to you for thirty-six years is answer enough.'

'You think I'm daft?'

'Well aren't you?'

'So who's carrying 900 sachets of salt, pepper and face-wipes?'

Next morning, at Gatwick, our weary group approached the 'green' channel with the usual statutory apprehension. As we entered, I sidled up to Jenny to ask her explanation if she was searched.

'Duty is not required on salt and pepper,' she whispered, in such a confident tone that I suspected she had been rehearsing throughout the nine-hour flight.

'It's not duty you should be worrying about,' I tormented her. 'Your problem's going to be import tax.'

Almost on cue, two chatting customs officers, who had been standing innocuously halfway down the hall, broke off their conversation and looked ominously towards us.

'Excuse me . . . sir,' one requested.

Sir? I silently echoed. What's all this with the 'Sir'? Surely he means 'Miss'? 'Miss' however, had sailed serenely on. My gut reaction was to yell out 'You have the wrong one! She's your man! Her with the half-ton of sugar and fifty pepperami sticks!'

Such a miscarriage of justice! I made a mental note to have a quick word with Martin. I mean, it's come to a sad state indeed when the police don't look after their own pensioners.

Albanian Interlude

Tell someone you are bound for Albania and you will receive one of the following responses:

(a) 'WHERE???' (This is not deafness but an incredulous disbelief.)
(b) 'What on earth d'you want to go there for?'
(c) 'You'll never get in (or out).'

There is also a fourth response but this will not be audible. It will consist of a discreet edging away. In addition, there will also be a sizable number who have either never heard of the place, or think it is a castle in a Frankenstein film. This reaction is partially understandable because the Albanians tend to be a bit choosey as to who they let in. The media are out straight away. (Come to think of it, this is no mean reason for going.) So are the police and service personnel, together with beatniks, scruffs and Americans of any sort.

My problem therefore, was what should I show under 'Occupation'? I guessed a 'retired' copper was, in Albanian eyes, as big an anathema as a 'serving' one. After all, the expression 'All coppers are bastards' doesn't actually differentiate between those who are still gainfully employed and those who are not. I did toy with the idea of 'Writer', but apart from sounding a little pretentious it seemed to border too close to 'media'.

So, if policeman and writer were out, what was in? I almost inserted 'Cellist'. It is true I have never played a cello in my life, but I thought it could be construed as a safe occupation in a closed country. On the other hand, anyone who could passably play 'Chopsticks' on comb-and-paper would be able to see through my musical ignorance within seconds.

'How about gardener?' suggested Joan. 'Your tomatoes aren't bad and you've at last got the hang of the compost heap.'

Of course! That was it! For the time I was in Albania, a gardener I would be.

I now realize that trips to such locations as Albania can present a severe shock to the system of the average traveller. I also now realize that package-tour operators are aware of this, and endeavour to prepare their clients in advance. For instance, take a typical flight to the average sun-and-beach holiday in, say, Spain or Greece. The trip will be so predictable as to be boring. Flight tickets are received well in advance, the passenger checks in, and, subject to the inevitable air traffic controllers' strike, the journey from beginning to end is relatively smooth. Now this predictability would be useless as a preparation for an Albanian trip. Tour operators have devised their own training course, and if my experience is anything to go by, it runs as follows.

Directions are sent only after your third agitated telephone call – even then there will be no tickets. This would be too reassuring. They just enclose a note with flight and check-in times. These will be incorrect. Your ticket, you are told, will be given to you by the firm's representative at the check-in desk, like a reward for your skill and determination in arriving there.

'Well, at least you won't have any tickets to lose,' said Joan, darkly hinting at a previous solo trip of mine. 'Just your passport,' she added, hinting at yet another.

The directions read that I was to report at 1.30 p.m. to the British Island Airways *south* terminal check-in at Gatwick for a 3 p.m. flight. At least, that is what they *wrote* to me. The message on my answerphone a few hours before the flight gave a different time, 12.30 p.m. for a 2 p.m. flight. Having planned a tight personal timetable for departure day, I was not best pleased at the short notice. But one adjusts, and I arrived at the south terminal exactly on cue. This uncharacteristic punctuality presented a problem; British Island Airways have no check-in desk at the *south* terminal. One discovers this after forty minutes of approaching every counter and asking every uniform in the place.

'Not here, sir,' sighed the bored enquiry girl. 'You'll need the train to the *north* terminal.'

All in all, not a bad start. Wrong time, wrong location and the journey not begun.

'You've cut it a little fine, sir,' reproved the Jules Verne representative as I breathlessly galloped, bags swinging, into the north terminal. 'No matter though . . .' he smiled, '. . . there's a two-hour delay.'

The next sixty minutes were particularly interesting as people dashed in from all over the country, with each 'hour-late' arrival now having appeared sixty minutes early, for a two-hour-delayed flight from the wrong terminal.

This delay at least gave me the opportunity to study my travelling companions. There were three separate tours with some forty travellers on each. In the main, we were a fairly innocuous bunch and I believe I was the only gardener. Jules Verne had suggested in their information pack (the one that sent us to the wrong terminal) that casual attire was the order of the day in Albania, with neither jacket nor tie a necessity. Most had conformed to this, with only a few going way over the top and looking like a seven-week sitter-in at the London School of Economics. The exceptions to this general air of dishevelment were Stanley and Reggie, two elderly, charming, tastefully-dressed English gentlemen from the Home Counties. They reminded me instantly of Basil Radford and Naunton Wayne in Hitchcock's film, *The Lady Vanishes*.

Eventually, the long single-deck bus chugged its way from the departure gate out across the tarmac and alongside our waiting BAC 1–11, where it remained, doors closed and stationary.

'We are sorry for this additional delay,' broke in a metallic voice, 'but we're not quite ready for you yet.'

'Still trying to find someone who's got the key and knows the way, I s'pose,' said a tired voice from somewhere behind.

However, the delay was short and our bus soon rolled up to the rear of the fuselage whilst another disgorged at the front. With no one to direct us, we each filed up the narrow staircase through the anus of the aircraft. My seat was in the second row, which was of course, in the front of the plane. 'Sod's law' then dictated that of the fifty or so souls who had entered from the front, thirty should be sitting at the back. I would estimate that some seventy-five of us met roughly halfway down the gangway.

Now passing *anyone* on a BAC 1–11 gangway turns by definition into an intimate act. To pass thirty is tantamount to an orgy – I was beginning to look for the grapes. It was at this stage that the stewardesses showed a great deal of common sense – they simply vanished until everyone had sat down of their own accord. I can only say that it seemed to work perfectly. Within minutes, some 110 people were sitting up at attention and waiting for the next announcement. 'Sitting up at attention' is a requirement of the 1–11 because the seats don't move. But then, very little else moves in the plane, so it is possible this has passed unnoticed.

Soon though, the initial shock faded as we stiffened our sinews in preparation for the next three and a half hours. With the seat in front nudging my knees and the table-flap cutting my waist, I was suddenly struck by a worrying thought. Should the plane ditch in the sea and we all drown, any subsequent retrieval of our bodies would present the mortician with massive interment problems. I mean, I had rigor mortis before we had crossed the channel. One hundred and ten stiffs fossilized in a sitting position would take a hell of a lot of wood.

One advantage to sitting up straight is that one can see more. I found my attention being drawn to my fellow-travellers' reading material. We had been warned that bibles and a whole host of other publications could not be taken into the country; I was therefore very interested to see that at least five passengers had played safe and were proudly displaying *The Ragged Trousered Philanthropists*. I bet it's a good few decades since five copies of that particular publication were seen in such a confined space. Speaking as someone who has made six attempts to read it, my admiration flowed.'

'We will be landing in Tirana in about fifteen minutes,' said the captain over the intercom. 'You will experience more vibration and noise than you have known on other landings. This is no cause for alarm. It is simply that Albanian tarmac does leave something to be desired.'

Well, he was most certainly right about that. We could have landed more smoothly on the Eiger.

'Did he say "vibration" or "disintegration"?' asked a questioning voice across the gangway.

I must say that runway dispelled my previous cynicism for the 1–11. Centurion tanks could have negotiated it no better. Knuckles whitened as we bounced merrily towards what appeared to be a neglected cricket pavilion. We had arrived.

We were ushered into a large, dimly-lit room in the pavilion. No light bulb in the whole of Albania appears stronger than forty watts . . . and there are very few of them. Jenny, our Albanian-speaking English guide, introduced us to Eddie, our English-speaking Albanian guide, who, in turn, introduced us to Bertie, our non-speaking driver.

'Eddie and Bertie?' marvelled a Welsh voice. 'They sound like fringe members of the Royal Family.'

'Customs,' announced Eddie, whose command of English was better than ninety-eight per cent of the rest of us. 'Pick up your cases, please.'

What he did *not* say was that for 110 people to clear the said customs would take two hours! Every bag, satchel and case was searched thoroughly. The main target of this quest seemed to be literature. ''Ave you books or magazines?' would be monotonously asked of each traveller as they laid bare their belongings. I carried a lurid American detective book that could never be construed as subversive. Well, only to the English language. Yet when I saw the furrowed brow of that uniformed examiner, I began to have doubts. Suddenly his attention was distracted, and his eyes lit up as he dived swiftly into the corner of my case. He muttered something in his own tongue that caused great excitement amongst his colleagues. They gathered swiftly around the pair of us. Clutching the offending item in his hand he thrust it quickly and questioningly into my face.

'This?' he demanded.

I suppose with its two prongs for a power-socket, a mosquito-killing tablet-burner *does* look a little sinister. As I had no great desire to become a political prisoner, I thought I had better make some attempt at an explanation. I held up my left arm and bent two fingers towards him, then wriggled them frantically.

'Buzz! Buzz! Buzz!' I mimicked. I then squiggled my hand around in the air for a moment before bringing it swiftly to rest on my own neck. 'PING!' I explained, as I quickly clapped my other hand over the imaginary bite in mock distress. The three examiners looked at me with some uncertainty. What, I wondered, was Albanian for 'Mosquitos! . . . the buggers always bite me!'

Finally, this seemingly endless search for books ceased and we were allowed to commence our tour. The darkness ensured we would see little of the countryside until next morning. In fact, the darkness ensured we would see little of anything. There is no doubt about it, Albanians definitely seem allergic to strong light. When I was a child during the 1939–45 war, we were told that eating carrots was good for our eyesight. If this claim is true, then Albanians must eat them by the truck-load, because I never saw *one* wearing spectacles.

We carried our cases to our bus and thirty minutes later arrived at our hotel in Durres. This was only marginally gloomier than the airport. The bus stopped in total blackness, in what I believe was the hotel driveway. Bertie raised the luggage flaps of the coach and we each felt blindly and hopefully for the familiar shape of our own suitcase. I 'touched-up' at least three people before I found mine; two of them seemed quite to enjoy it. The giggles, squeaks and sighs of the great blind bag-search then gave way to bangs, groans and threats as people now fell over them.

We had been told weeks previously that a torch would prove a most useful asset and we had all sensibly packed one. In fact, without *exception* we had packed one . . . and without exception, we had packed it safely in our suitcases – the very article we could not now find because we had no torch. I finally entered the hotel foyer (with the wrong case of course), and joined the bartering group in the luggage exchange. Within minutes we were each happily reunited with our baggage.

Durres is a small coastal town on the Adriatic, some twenty miles from Tirana, the capital of Albania, and our hotel was situated almost at the water's edge. True, this was an excellent setting, but it did not make for a restful night. Every few seconds, the rolling waves could clearly be heard in every bedroom. This would have been quite tolerable, except for my bed – it could almost hold a conversation. It was the only bed I had ever known that squeaked when someone walked across the room. It would have sent honeymooners mad. Every move, every breath, and I swear, every thought, caused a squeak to originate somewhere in that sagging frame. The nocturnal sound-track went something as follows: squeak-crash, squeak-crash, squeak-crash, until finally, at 1.45 a.m., I gave in and moved my mattress to the floor. The bed then squeaked another six times in temper before I finally lost consciousness.

A little after 6.30 a.m. I woke to the rhythm of the waves and the occasional squeak. I lifted the blind. The morning was beautiful. There was not a cloud in sight, and beyond the rippling shallows the sea was mill-pond still. There were two distant ships, and some fifty yards of coarse clean sand lay between the hotel patio and the water. This was it! A clear, crisp, late October swim. It would set me up for the whole holiday. Slipping into my swim-shorts, I padded out of the hotel. The first surprise was the temperature. It may have been the Adriatic but it was definitely *not* warm – and that was just the sand!

The nearer I went to the water, the more my enthusiasm receded, but finally it was toe-dipping time. Bravely stifling a scream, I decided I had absorbed all the fresh air and invigoration that a mature chap could require on such a holiday. With one wet foot, I turned towards the hotel. To my horror, I saw at least eight travelling-companions waving supportively from their balconies, all telling me what a brave soul I was. I am sure people win medals that way. There was nothing else for it but a holding-of-the-breath and a diving-in.

Get it over quick, was to be the plan. Dive under the first little wave, swim round in a small circle, then OUT.

Almost as soon as I had made the plan, I had to abandon it. There was no way I could dive in at that location – the water was too shallow. I would need to walk out a few more feet. I did. Then I walked out a few more feet. Then I walked out a few more yards. A hundred yards off-shore it was still only knee-deep. At that rate I would reach Italy before I could swim. I don't know if the

Albanian navy has submarines, but if it has, they must be crewed by water-voles and run on roller-skates.

The persistent shallows made inroads into my courage. After ten minutes in the water, I had still not reached the point that all male swimmers dislike, the moment when the first shock of cold water swirls exploratively around the genitals. This dousing is always good for two sharp intakes of breath, twenty seconds on tip-toe and a month's impotence. Finally, as Italy loomed, the bottom fell away. The only reason mine did not join it was because it was too constricted by cold.

After lots of splashing, a few quick back-strokes and an airy wave to the watchers from the balconies, I made tracks for that long walk back. This is the moment when all swimmers lie outrageously. 'How was it? Cold I bet!' will be the calls from the watchers. 'No,' we laugh gaily, 'it was really lovely. Once you get in it is actually quite warm. Go on, try it,' we say encouragingly.

I suppose this is basically an admission that we have been a bit of a prat and we would dearly love someone else to be as big a fool as we were. Anyway, on this occasion it worked, for at least two of my support group appeared on the beach, if only for an extended paddle. The interesting thing was that they too swore it was warm, although their stay was even shorter than mine.

Soon after breakfast, our guide, Eddie, really came into his own. The meal had introduced us to the general pattern of most Albanian food, i.e., it was not as bad as it looked, but then that would have been difficult. Eddie was fiercely Albanian, his knowledge of his country was truly impressive and he kept me fascinated as he recounted its numerous conquerors. He began in the Bronze Age, when it was known as Illyria, then ranged through such invaders as Phoenicians, Greeks, Romans, Byzantines, Bulgars, Visigoths, Ostrogoths, Normans, Crusaders, Huns, Slavs, Turks, Italians and Germans – who doubtless, even in those days, left their towels on the deckchairs.

Now that is a pretty impressive bunch. About the only ones missing were the Flat Earth Society, Millwall Supporters' Club and of course, the Brits. Speaking *as* a Brit, I felt quite left out of it. With our imperial track record, however had we missed it? Yet to be fair, after twenty minutes in the place, one does begin to wonder just what the attraction is. Mountainous it may be – Shangrila it ain't.

This constant occupation by one mob or another has understandably made the Albanians insular, suspicious and more than a mite bristly. Within the last forty-five years they seem to have fallen out with everyone at one time or another, yet this does not seem to bother them, and they seem to look upon the tourist with great indifference. Why should they take any other attitude? Especially with us – we haven't had diplomatic relations with them for forty years.

After two days touring the countryside, one receives the impression that Albanians will be quite disappointed if they are *not* invaded. After all, they have made such preparations to combat it; firstly, they have increased their population from below two million to more than three in less than two generations (probably all those dark nights); secondly, their army, people's police and many other assorted uniforms seem to be everywhere, and finally, they have, I swear, more concrete pill-boxes than people. When in doubt, erect a pill-box! In England, we have thistles in the hedgerows; in Albania, they have twenty-ton concrete blocks. I saw fifteen of them in one field – it was as if they were expecting Attila. If cavalry comes back in fashion the Albanians will be a superpower.

Perhaps the most puzzling aspect of most totalitarian states is their apparent obsession with their leaders' little homilies, or in the Albanian case, their former and now deceased leader, Enver Hoxha, who died in 1985. His picture, statues and quotations are everywhere.

Take Albanian museums, for example. They are new, well-designed and aesthetically pleasing. It is natural for the visitor to give at least an enquiring glance as to the builder. Sure enough, there will be the inevitable five lines of unreadable inscription, preceded by a picture and followed by the name – Enver Hoxha. Those of us not familiar with the language and politically ignorant could easily be forgiven for thinking that Enver Hoxha was 'Painter and Decorator to the Nation'.

Having left Durres for Tirana, I wondered what to expect. In fact, Tirana was just like Durres: dimly lit, no shops, no traffic and pictures galore of good old Enver. I must admit, I did enjoy the absence of traffic. It was lovely to walk in the road with only cyclists to worry about. The central square in Tirana is impressive, with wide roads and acres of space. At one of its main junctions stands a policeman. Every two minutes he blows furiously on his whistle and waves like mad at the pedestrians and cyclists, as if practising for the day when he has some real traffic. As personal memories of a London traffic-point flooded back, I wondered what the Albanian might be for 'Enjoy it while you can, mate.'

The Hotel Tirana stands in an ideal position facing the

city square. It was, we were assured, a *first-class* hotel. After Durres, any hotel that offered a non-squeak bed was going to be first-class. I hurried to my front-facing seventh-floor room and vigorously pushed the mattress up and down. Not bad. Not bad at all. If an Albanian bed is the first check, then an Albanian bathroom is a very close second. I switched on the dim light and found it was a bathroom in name only; it was, in fact, a bathroom with no bath. Not to worry, how about the shower? A shower cubicle there certainly was – but no shower head. No matter, I can stand under the pipe. How about the lavatory? Yes, a lavatory! No seat . . . but then one can't have everything. The wash-basin appeared a little battered but nevertheless serviceable. Ah, no plug.

I often wonder what happens to these plugs. Who has them? I first ran across this phenomenon forty years ago in the army and it has persisted ever since. Did, I wonder, just one person in Salamanca Barracks, Aldershot, begin the whole process by stealing a solitary plug in 1948? Then, Pandora-like, the plug-stealing plague-germ escaped and ever since that day, a chain-reaction of plugless basins has spread world-wide? If this is indeed the case, then I know the culprit. He was a fat lad from Bolton called Blenkinsop, who should now be damned for the inconvenience he has caused millions.

Having paused to curse Blenkinsop, I then stood bathless, showerless, seatless and plugless, evaluating the situation. It was only then I discovered that all these misfortunes were purely academic, because there was no water. It is strange how the absence of water reduces all other problems to trivia. I did possess two-thirds of a bottle of natural mineral water but I was not sure how far this would stretch. I could clean my teeth and have the shallowest of washes, but could I, as my Aunt Violet used to say, 'wash all my joints'? I doubted it. The one bright spot was my now fortuitous constipation. I would have hated to have used my precious bottled water on one heartbreaking flush.

It was during this inventory of the bathroom that I first noticed the toilet roll. It was reassuringly there, but it was a suspicious shade of greyish dark brown. It had obviously been recycled, but just how *efficiently* recycled and recycled from *what*, I dreaded to contemplate.

I joined the ten-minute queue at reception to report my misfortune.

'Nix wat-ter . . . one hour, yes?' asked the indifferent girl clerk, neatly pre-empting my complaint.

'One hour, yes,' I agreed, as I joined the rest of the seventh-floor guests in a sixty-minute walkabout.

It was during this group stroll that the subject of earthquakes arose. These disasters are by no means unknown in the country, and one of our party caused me no little concern as he aired his knowledge about the regularity of these quakes and the general low standard of Albanian buildings. This was, I thought, an ill-chosen topic for a seventh-floor guest.

It was some seventy-five minutes later that we returned to the hotel.

'Wat-ter . . . vere soon,' called the now-happier clerk. 'Vere soon indeed,' she beamed.

Noticing a double queue for the two tiny lifts, I chose the stairs. I peered hopefully into the gloom of the bathroom and turned on both basin taps – 'Nix wat-ter!'

I decided to wait for a while, and went to the bedroom window, which offered me an excellent view over Tirana's roof-tops, clear across to the far mountains. I must have spent some minutes just lost in the view, when I was aware of a distant tremor. What was it that fool said about Albanian buildings? The tremors then increased dramatically and the very floor shook; bangs and bumps resounded and there was a loud, hissing scream, like a jet plane landing. My first thought was to leap from the window, but this quickly subsided as I realized that the noise, terrifying though it may have been, was confined to the bathroom. Distant cheers along the corridor announced the welcome return of the wat-ter. The deep rumbles and tremors soon gave way to an alarming but localized 'Cha-chang! Cha-chang! Cha-chang!' with each pipe twanging like a bowstring. If this was a regular occurrence, it explained the absence of bath, shower-head, lavatory-seat and plug. They had clearly disintegrated.

With a mental apology to Blenkinsop, I undressed and turned on the shower pipe. What first emerged from this pipe was not water but a fine spray of rust-dust, quickly followed by two cockroaches and a quantity of mud. However, this again quickly changed to a reddy-brown mixture, which in turn diluted slowly into a reasonably clear liquid. The water may have cleared but it certainly hadn't warmed; well, a cold shower was better than no shower. I took a deep breath, kicked a cockroach into the drain-hole and braved the splattering torrent. It was not a lot of fun.

Perhaps a word should be written here about Albanian hotel lifts. Marginally smaller than the average car boot, they will hold a maximum of five thin people, or three fat ones, or two fat ones in overcoats. Anything over that and buzzers and bells will drive you mad. Unfortunately, difficulties do not cease with their capacity. No, their main problem is their sheer inordinate cussedness in doing their own thing. Many nations have national lotteries – Albanians have lift buttons. Whatever number is pressed on the panel will have little or no connection with the eventual destination. 'Ground' can be anywhere between 'Basement' and 'Roof', and occasionally a lift will stop at every level *except* the one required. It will then pop up and down for ten minutes or so until the occupants forget which floor they wanted in the first place.

I once pressed the call-button on the dining-room level in Tirana, and the door slowly opened to reveal the same sardine-packed quintet who had left the level some few minutes earlier. It was too full to enter, so I 'bon-voyaged' them and waited for its return. It returned well enough. In fact it returned three times in the next four minutes. Unfortunately it still contained the same five people.

'We are just going for a little ride this morning,' explained Reggie from somewhere in its depths. 'I suspect we'll be back for lunch.'

It is soon noticeable that no matter how many floors to a hotel, Albanians rarely ride in their lifts. They probably don't have the time. The exception to this was in Durres, where we actually had a lift *attendant! Not* a sensible posting, I would say. Apart from reducing capacity by twenty-five per cent, he probably hadn't been home for two months. In fact, one member of our party swore that four complete strangers entered a lift in Shkoder and actually emerged as engaged couples. Personally, I thought that was a little over the top.

Shkoder is the most northerly town of any size in the country and our schedule allowed for a little under a day to be spent there. Two hours after our arrival a steady downpour began, which increased in volume throughout the night. When we left the following morning, it looked as if it would rain forever. The two dry hours we did experience I found particularly interesting. We had arrived a little before 6 p.m. and dinner was not scheduled until 8 p.m. – just enough time for a quick exploration.

A large gathering of people, some two or three hundred strong, had assembled across a road junction some three minutes' walk from the hotel. Believing such gatherings to be illegal, I made tracks to discover the motivation of this crowd. Although they were spilled over pavement and road, the absence of traffic rendered this safe, with the exception of the cyclists of course, who simply threaded their way through.

This short walk was not without incident, because for the first time in Albania, I was besieged by children.

''Allo,' greeted one, in excellent English. 'What is your name?'

'Harry,' I replied. 'And yours?'

'Michael – or Mickey as you say – yes?'

'Yes,' I agreed. 'And the other names?' I pointed generally to the dozen or so youngsters, around ten to twelve years old, who hovered nervously a few yards away.

He then recited me a list of first – I hesitate to say *Christian* – names which appeared to me so English that I am sure he made them up; probably the most surprising of these was 'Alfie'.

'Where did you learn such good English?' I complimented him.

'At school,' he shrugged, and although he pretended indifference, he could not hide his pleasure at my praise. 'Do you have pens?' he asked.

'Pens?' I echoed.

For some silly reason, the only pen I could readily think of was an animal pen. I had this vague idea he thought I was a farmer. Before I could show myself a complete cretin, he made a pretend scrawl on the palm of his hand.

'Ah!' I exclaimed, the penny finally dropping. 'You mean *pen* pens! . . . Yes?'

'Yes!' he agreed eagerly.

I was so delighted to have guessed that I recklessly fumbled for the only pen I had with me on holiday. This movement was the signal for the rest of his troop to show interest, and by the time the pen was in his hand, three friends were on his back, each madly scrambling for a thirty-pence black Bic-Biro. Soon all twelve had joined the fray, although I was pleased to see my new acquaintance retain possession. How to separate them was my next thought. Of course! The eternal boiled sweets! Joan *would* have been proud.

'Whoa! Whoa! Whoa!' I cried. 'Here, have a sweet.' I offered the open tin to the company of losers.

In spite of the fact they had just fought like jackals for my pen, they politely waited their turn before thrusting a small grimy hand into the tin. Then each did a strange thing. Not one of them put the sweet into his mouth. Instead it was placed carefully into a pocket and I was thanked profusely (I believe) in Albanian.

This action was to be repeated several times before we left the country – never did I see a child eat an offered sweet. One member of our party distributed several chocolate bars to the children. They were suspicious at first but quickly caught on. Yet no matter how ragged, shoeless or thin they were, not one child as much as opened a wrapper.

As the children disappeared with their sweets, I reached the junction. If anything, the crowd was now greater. Just *what* were they doing? The answer I discovered, was not a lot – it was simply that it was a *Sunday*. Now in Albania, if Mondays to Saturdays are boring, Sundays are excruciating! Then, just to add charm to the situation, it began to rain. The now damp citizens had turned out to stroll up the streets, to see and be seen, to promenade, to gossip. Well, at least the men had. The only two shops that were open and, by Albanian standards, brightly illuminated, were both barber-shops. Although the customers were all male, at least two of the actual barbers were women. Well, that was it; that was Shkoder. That was the uptown, downtown and night-life; even with a couple of lady barbers it seemed a long way from Sin City. As if to prove a point, the rain began to bounce off the pavement. I felt sorry for the promenaders. Their creased, bell-bottomed-trousered suits made the whole thing look like a 1972 road navvies' reunion. Now the rain had even put paid to that; heaven knows where they went to, but within minutes all had faded quickly into the wet night.

Of course, I may have misjudged the natives over their rapid disappearance. I had assumed that the sudden heavy rain was the cause, yet moments later, martial music blared from the spray of loudspeakers and soon a powerful metallic oration began. This declamation continued from the speakers for some thirty minutes, with just the occasional musical interlude. Whether it was the rain or the political broadcast that had cleared the street, I could not be sure, but there was not a bell-bottom to be seen.

That evening, our group played for time and lingered leisurely over dinner. After all, with the night now pouring hard and dark, there was little else to do. Suddenly, Jenny, our Albanian-speaking English guide, glided swiftly into the dining-room. Discreetly approaching each table, she appeared to utter a few confidential words. Once she had finished, each diner slid back his or her chair and left the room. The whole thing appeared devious, and realizing I was sitting at the last table she would approach, I began to anticipate her message. Were we to assist in some espionage plot? Perhaps even now there was some poor bedraggled agent sheltering in a dark Albanian doorway. Could we now be his only chance of reaching England, home and safety? Could *this* have been why the loudspeakers were so persistent? Perhaps it was not a political broadcast at all, but an urgent find-this-man-at-all-costs appeal. Yes, that was it! What else could it be? A sort of 'Spy Who Came In From The Cold and Wet'! Well you can certainly count on me, ma'am!

'I wonder if you could all do something important for me?' she whispered. 'Discreetly though,' she added.

We each leaned forward eagerly. It was obvious that even without consultation we had all arrived at the same conclusion.

'Yes, gel,' snapped a now-alert Reggie. 'Name it.'

'In the far room – ' she nodded in the general direction – 'is an Albanian pop-group, and they are very upset that no one has come to listen to them. It would be a loss of face to them if they knew I was rounding you up. So will you just sidle in there and form an audience?'

No one turned a hair and within seconds we had switched from saving our man in Albania to cheering up a despairing pop-group. What it is to be British and abroad!

I must confess I found the mere thought of such a group daunting. What would it sound like? My first glance was not reassuring; with drum, guitar, accordion and sax, they looked a combination of everything I do not hold dear.

'I don't really know what I'm doing watching an

Albanian pop-group,' murmured a puzzled Stanley, 'I don't even like British ones.'

I knew the feeling. As someone who had not bought a record since Billy Cotton died, I viewed the commencement of the concert with no little apprehension. It would be nice to say that as the group began to play our fears melted into a universal musical appreciation, but sadly I cannot. They were as awful as we had feared they might be, except they played each tune longer and louder than expected.

In these situations, I have found the best policy is to move quickly. After all, the band will not improve, it will only get worse; therefore the time to leave is as soon as possible, or before your departure is too obvious. One can ease comfortably from a crowd of forty or so, perhaps with slightly less ease from, say, twenty-five. But when it gets down to ten, to leave seems an act of paramount cowardice.

Minutes later, I was halfway up the stairs. Third one out and thirty-eight to go. I did not escape unpunished. As I entered my room for an enforced early night, I reached for the switch that should have bathed the room in its customary forty-watt glow. The switch clicked on but the light did not. Instead, and I hope by eerie coincidence, the martial music roared into life. I walked to the window and stared out into the dark, monsoon-like street. Except for the rain, nothing moved. Was our man still out there, hiding in the dark? Lucky sod! If he wasn't careful, there could well be forty-one others about to join him.

Next morning at breakfast, the fifteen stalwarts who had remained at the concert regaled us with tales like survivors of some blitz. We were impressed by their loyalty, if not their sensitivity. We had been due to visit a mountain-top castle that morning, but the incessant rain had made stony paths dangerous and turned grassy paths into a morass. Instead, we visited the local cultural centre, which displayed traditional Albanian handicrafts. There was an incident there that typifies the dilemma this emerging country now faces. Our group had meandered around the various displays which also sported the types of craft tools used, many of which were obviously unchanged since the dark ages. I left the shop with a pleasant young Devonian woman and we chatted generally about the skill of the craftsmen who still used these old tools.

As we stepped on to the pavement, we paused to allow a bent old Albanian woman to pass. She was dressed entirely in black from shawl to shoes. She was small of stature and sunk of face, and showed a curiosity towards us common in elderly Albanians. It was raining as hard as ever and her curiosity increased when my young companion removed a folded automatic umbrella from her handbag. It was instantly apparent that the old lady could not fathom its function. The girl then raised the brolly and clicked the spring. The resulting magical transformation from a small compact article into a fully opened functional umbrella astounded the old woman and caused her to collide with the only lamp-post in the street. As someone who has never yet mastered the rotten things, I appreciated her astonishment.

I later recounted this incident to Reggie and Stanley, and in turn they told me of their experience on our Saturday evening in Tirana. They had naïvely asked our guides to recommend a restaurant in town, only to be told there was no such thing as a restaurant in Albania. So after their evening meal in our hotel, the pair went off on a walkabout around the back streets of Tirana, which at least has the one advantage over many western cities, in that its streets are safe. Hearing *traditional* music coming from the direction of a closed door, they peeked in, hoping it might be a bar of some description.

To their horror, they found they had opened a door immediately behind the top table of a wedding party. Even worse, almost everyone at the reception had spotted them before the pair had time to realize their mistake. Instantly, several top table guests, including the groom and a few important elders, seized the pair and propelled them into the room. Both had visions of at least an international incident, or at worst, bloody murder. In fact, their seizure had been made with great delight by the guests, for the unexpected arrival of such strangers at a wedding was construed as good luck. Of course, the luck was not quite so good for two original guests, who were then thrown off the top table in order to make room, but at least the Britons kept their throats intact. Which, judging by the amount that was subsequently poured down them, was fortuitous.

My few days in Albania did *not* pass quickly and as we drove through the unrelenting rain to the airport, I wondered why. The country did have a fascination, though – it was like a time capsule permanently entrenched in the early 1930s; yet one wonders why the colour and the gaiety of other Mediterranean countries had not overflowed its borders. There were many things that would stay in my mind. For instance, the hotel room-maid who discovered a *Cosmopolitan* magazine in the rubbish bin. She secreted it swiftly under her clothing as if it was the blueprint of the Star Wars defence system, and looking anxious and excited at the same time she scuttled into the store-cupboard at the end of the seventh floor.

Then there were the two old ladies in a field that we passed. One sat cross-legged and patient on the wet ground, whilst the other strapped a huge bundle of tree branches across the sitter's back. Each branch appeared larger than either of the two women. They both seemed about seventy years of age, but then so do most Albanians over forty-five.

Finally, there were the children, of whom so many had a dullness about them that I had not experienced before. The 'Artful Dodger' in Shkoder was like a breath of air; I should think that lad will go a long way in Albania. Though he will doubtless go further still if he leaves, in every sense.

On returning to Tirana airport, the traveller will need to change his or her Albanian currency (leks) back into sterling since no leks are allowed to leave the country. Not that they would be any use, even if you managed it. The Dow Jones index would not give a quiver if everyone took out a truckful. It is then that you realize the full cost of your stay. I changed ten pounds when I entered the country and I received £5.25p back when I *left!* Running expenses for three days: three bottles of wine (not bad), three bottles of beer (not good), two litres of natural mineral water (boring) and two Albanian brandies (made that morning). On the other hand, I would have swopped the lot for one really *hot* meal and a bath.

After the currency change, we were at last reunited with our passports, which seemed to hold a fascination for anyone in authority. Hotel clerks swapped them for your room key. Our flight was announced and we filed wearily through all the usual controls. Our last journey would be to hike across the two hundred yards of tarmac to our waiting aircraft. The rain had been unrelenting now for more than twenty-four hours and we scurried, bent almost double, for the sanctuary of the aircraft and a truly bright light. On reaching the steps, there appeared to be a hold-up just inside the door of the plane, which neatly left us soaking outside. Slowly, oh so slowly, the line eased up the steps and into the body of the craft. It was there that the cause of our final delay was apparent. A cherubic-faced People's Policeman was having a final scrutiny of our passports – and, of course, everyone had stowed them safely away not ten minutes before.

'Strange nation, old chap,' I heard Stan murmur thoughtfully. 'They don't seem to want us in. Then they don't seem to want us out.' He then sidled closer and whispered confidentially: 'As well you told 'em you're a gardener, though. If you'd told 'em you're a plumber, you'd be here forever.'

Perish the thought.

A Slow Boat in China

'Why on earth d'you want to go to China?' asked Joan incredulously. 'You don't even like sweet-and-sour pork.'

'It's *because* I don't like sweet-and-sour pork that I am going,' I replied. 'I just thought perhaps it's time I tried something else. You never know. I might even like it.'

'Then why don't you go down to Tonkin's Takeaway? It'd be a whole lot quicker – and infinitely cheaper.'

'Tonkin's Takeaway smells . . . so are you coming or not?'

'To Tonkin's?'

'You know full well I am talking about *China*. Quick, make your mind up, yes or no?'

'What's involved?'

'A plane to Peking, three more internal flights, one overnight train-sleeper and a couple of days on a Yangtse steamer. The whole tour then finishes in Hong Kong. Coming?'

I knew the conversation had now reached Joan's basic formula questions for any distant trip:

(1) Would we have to share a bathroom with anyone else?
(2) Would we have to share a bedroom with any creatures? Particularly the eight, four, or worst of all, no-legged, variety?

(3) Is the temperature over seventy-five Fahrenheit and do they eat cats?

She was exactly on cue. 'How about bathrooms? Would we have to share?'

'Nah! I doubt if we'd even *have* a bathroom, so there's no point worrying over sharing.'

'. . . And creatures?'

Now some folk can say 'creatures' and conjure up something cuddly and furry. But Joan's 'creatures' tend to come from the Black Lagoon.

'Creatures, as you call them, there certainly will be.'

'This is not sounding good,' she murmured.

'It gets worse before it gets better,' I pointed out. 'It's also hot and they eat cats.'

'That's it, mate,' she said emphatically. 'You're on your own. Have fun.'

As a result of that conversation, three months later, together with thirty-four other hardy souls, I was looking for my luggage in the arrival lounge in Peking airport. I now realize it is a good idea to start this baggage search just as soon as you land in China – it gets it out of your system. During my fifteen days in China, I saw my luggage about three times. The first was when it lay apparently abandoned in the corner of an overgrown army airfield in Xian, where a nervous young soldier threatened to shoot an even more nervous old policeman, for even showing an interest in his own suitcase. On the second occasion, I was actually allowed a brief reunion with it.

This was at 6.45 a.m. on a wet, dark, Chungking morning. This concession was to enable me to carry it down 250 crumbling, unlit steps, to a smelly, sweating, Yangtse steamer. The guide pointed out that when the necessity arose to hump any article great distances, it was a quaint Chinese practice to reunite travellers with their cases. My third and final sighting was when it lay on the back of a ramshackle lorry that was just about making its way east along the Hongqiao Road in Shanghai. Sadly, our coach was travelling west at the time.

After a while, one becomes quite used to living out of one's hand-luggage and wearing the same shirt and underpants for days on end. This gives you the added advantage of being able to return home after two weeks' holiday with a suitcase full of clean clothes. Do not misunderstand, this absence of luggage is never *permanent*; the Chinese are scrupulously honest, and your cases will always catch up with you in Hong Kong. Sadly, this is rather perverse, Hong Kong being the one place in the world where it is possible to pop out for a few minutes before breakfast and return, half an hour later, rigged out for Ascot.

This baggage problem begins from the very moment of arrival in China, yet there had been no indication prior to landing that our suitcases were to have a different tour to ourselves. It had been a normal package-tour flight in every respect. It was two hours late, the film had broken down, the kid in the seat behind kept banging the back of my head and I discovered those travelling with a different travel company had paid twenty quid less than I had. In other words, just an everyday package-tour trip. Then, after the usual bureaucratic formalities, the information screen announced our baggage would be arriving on number one carousel. It had been a long journey and everyone gathered around the creaking mobile circuit and stared glazed-eyed at the flapped entrance. We were still staring some twenty minutes later.

Suddenly a few local people scurried to the second carousel some twenty yards away. There was mass indecision at first. Then a smart-suited, slightly-built young Chinese fellow pointed out that the information screen now showed that number two carousel was to display our cases. There were a few impatient sighs as the main body of people transferred their attention to this second carousel.

It was whilst waiting there that I realized my young Chinese informant had some two dozen identical copies of himself, clustered all about him. These young business men, returning no doubt from some engagement abroad, were identical in every respect; dress, features, build and hair could not be separated. Neither could their height, about five feet six inches. I had yet to discover that seven-eighths of the entire Chinese nation were slim, dark-haired and five feet six inches. Heaven only knows what they do with their fatties, but in fifteen days I never saw one.

At the end of the further half-hour that we spent gathered around number two carousel, our cases bounced merrily out on to number *three*. Now the seasoned China traveller (i.e. anyone who has been there longer than two days), after hearing the cases were due in at number one, would have gone immediately to number three. Yet these niggles simply do not bother the Chinese. Hold-ups, restraints and protractions, they feel, are an unavoidable part of life, so why worry? The rest of the world may fume, but not the Chinese. Nowadays they have a saying that even Confucius would have envied. 'No problems, just changes.' This means that to have a problem is a loss of face. Problems, therefore, are not allowed. When you are on a train to Peking and your baggage is on a boat to Shanghai, you may understandably think you have a problem. Not so – in China this is simply a change.

The Russian-built Friendship Hotel in Peking is quite a pleasant hotel – what am I saying! In comparison to many other Chinese hotels, the Friendship is one of the six all-time greats! (Do not be misled by this equation; in relation to the average Chinese hostelry, my bike-shed is the Taj Mahal.) Now although the Friendship certainly has its faults – for example, a moonlit roof-top cocktail bar, that serves its drinks in white plastic cups – it does possess an Olympic-sized, open-air swimming-pool. Not only that; because of a late afternoon chill, I had the whole pool to myself. Such luxury! There was a sign over the entrance that later in the tour would have caused me great amusement – 'CERTIFICATE OF HEALTH REQUIRED'. What *was* a certificate of health, and how, in a country where hygiene appears non-existent, could one be purchased?

At that stage, I had not the faintest idea about such a document. Neither, it seemed, had the attendant. Either that, or she was so delighted to receive her first customer of the day that she wasn't asking. She simply smiled, and then picked the precise moment that I had stripped to the buff to stroll in and mop over the floor. I was not altogether displeased; neither, I hope, was the attendant.

The walk from the hotel to the pool and back was about 150 yards. During the minute or two that took, I must have passed a dozen or so Chinese of varying ages. At least a third of them – and of both sexes – cleared their throats noisily and had a thundering good spit. By the second day, I had the impression that the three essential Chinese functions are breathing, walking and spitting – and not necessarily in that order.

'Why do they spit everywhere?' I later asked a local guide.

'What do *you* do if you want to spit?' he replied.

It was a topic to which I had never before given serious thought. I should have.

'Well . . . er . . . I use my handkerchief . . . or a tissue, I s'pose,' I shrugged.

'E-zactly!' he exploded triumphantly, '. . . and that is what puzzles many Chinese.'

'*Puzzles* them?'

'Yes, puzzles them. We spit it out – you take it home. When you get it home, what do you do with it? Do you bank it, make things out of it, or bury it? Is it valuable?'

I dropped the subject.

My room in the Friendship was good. Joan would have been particularly delighted with the bathroom – not a 'creature' in sight. After my swim, I was hungry for my first real Chinese meal. I must say it looked very pretty and consisted of some sixteen to twenty small dishes, placed on a large, flat, circular disc that, in turn, took up most of the area of an even larger, twelve-seater, circular table. This disc revolved, so after you had helped yourself, you spun it on to the next person who desired beans, sea-cucumber or strange brown squiggly things.

The big problem with this system was that if you missed anything, it had to complete a circuit of eleven other diners before it returned. Whenever this happened, there was always a fat lady opposite who would infuriatingly swoop up the particular morsel that had escaped your first trawl.

In addition there was the serious offence of leaving the serving spoon protruding from the dish. The usual result of this misdemeanour would be the scything down of every glass and bottle on the table. It was something I never seemed to learn. My personal record was set in Xian, where, whilst slightly preoccupied, I demolished two bottles of beer, one and a half bottles of red wine and four glasses of mineral water.

The early general opinion of our group on the food was favourable, and I immediately realized that if thirty-four assorted people found it acceptable, it would be a mean-minded, contrary sod who disagreed. But then, my mother always said I was. The proof of this particular pudding was therefore *not* in the eating. My loss of fourteen pounds in fifteen days tells its own story.

Next morning, the tour began in earnest. Harvey, our English courier, was to remain with us throughout. We were also accompanied, at least until Hong Kong, by Rose Li, a lovely young Chinese 'liaison' officer. These people can be invaluable in communist countries where bureaucracy is usually mindblowing; as if to prove the point, we were in need of her services on our very first morning.

A lady of our group fell and sustained a nasty injury which left her unable to walk and in need of hospital treatment. It was decided to fly the poor woman and her husband, first to Hong Kong, then to Britain. The problem was that we had a group visa for thirty-four people, but we were then down to thirty-two. In addition, our two unfortunates were hoping to leave the country without a visa! Two serious violations of the visa regulations! It took the fair Rose a day and a half to sort out that little lot. Besides Harvey and Rose, we would also pick up a regional guide in most cities and provinces. These were always very good and would answer most questions – except about the Cultural Revolution.

The first full day of our tour was to take in Ming's Tomb and the Great Wall. Now I must confess, although I have always been fascinated by the Wall, I am a Philistine as regards Ming. I had certainly heard of him, who hasn't, but I had somehow never placed him as the Emperor of China. In my mind, Ming was the skinny, bearded, sinister-looking weirdo who was always trying to kill Flash Gordon in the Saturday morning 'tuppeny-rush' cinemas of my childhood. Whether this clouded my judgement, I am not sure; but to me, Ming's Tomb had all the glamour of a wartime deep shelter.

The Wall, on the other hand, was everything I had expected, although I felt it was a little ironic that a construction designed solely to keep out the hordes was now responsible for fetching them back. I had a feeling that if I walked long enough along the Wall, I would be bound to meet someone I know. It is that sort of wall.

The journey from our hotel to the Wall took about two hours and was my first introduction to Chinese traffic. About eighty per cent of all Chinese vehicles are cycles, which flood every road in their thousands, so that they resemble tinkling, multi-coloured rivers. In spite of such high numbers of cyclists, there are still enough other forms of wheeled traffic to cause horrendous jams. We were very fortunate in the location of our hotel, situated as it was out in the north-west suburb of Peking. This meant that we usually missed the worst of the traffic. Throughout the two weeks, my admiration of our bus drivers' patience increased daily. There appeared to be no system or discipline to the traffic; even old men, with old horses and carts, would do incredibly silly things. Yet other than a token hoot, our drivers took it calmly in their stride.

However, this tranquillity does not transmit itself to the traffic wardens. (I use the term 'traffic warden' in the absence of a suitable translation, because they are a very long way from our interpretation of 'warden'.) These gentlemen are retired pensioners who feel they would still like to be of use to the community, so they are given a badge, no training whatever and turned loose. As far as I could see, their prime functions were to scream, shout and thump cyclists – in all three, they excel.

If traffic is undisciplined, pedestrians are expendable. For example, I never saw anything in China that would prevent any person or any vehicle falling down a hole in the road or pavement; six inches or six feet, it made no difference. It was a hole, and light or dark, you were expected to see it. On our second night, as we returned from the theatre, one of our group walked into an overflow pipe that protruded from a wall, six feet above a darkened pavement. It opened up his scalp like a razor. In London he could sue; in Peking he was a bloody fool for not seeing it. On the other hand, I suppose a thousand million, five-feet-six-inch, slightly-built Chinese could have walked underneath it with inches to spare.

Next morning, I had the feeling that at least half of that thousand million were queueing around Tiananmen Square, for the somewhat dubious pleasure of seeing the embalmed body of Chairman Mao, as it lay in the huge and grand Mao's Mausoleum. At least, that is what it looked like as we alighted from our bus.

'It's not *that* important,' I said curtly to Harvey. 'After all, the bloke's dead. I have no desire to queue for half a day to see a corpse.'

'But we do *not* queue,' he explained.

'Don't queue?' I pointed at the thousands lining the square – the largest in the world.

'That's right,' he emphasized. 'Tourists have priority. They go straight to the front.'

'No wonder the Boxers had a rebellion!' I said. 'I should think that lot will have the right needle if they have been queueing for six hours and a bus load of white-kneed Brits calmly walk to the front!'

'They will accept it happily, you'll see.'

They did too – although exactly what we were all doing there, I have since wondered. The dead Mao certainly looked better than, say, the late live Brezhnev, but that was about all. He still looked less well than any of his statues.

It had been a long two days. There had been the food, the Forbidden City and the Summer Palace. We had fought the War of Liberation, the Civil War and the Cultural Revolution, we had explored Ming's and Mao's tombs and assailed the Great Wall. With twelve days now to go, I was experiencing the first flutters of battle fatigue.

In order to unwind, Harvey, our courier, had suggested a Peking Duck dinner at one of the best restaurants in town. The coach had taken us from the Friendship Hotel across the city to Fuxingmen (I kid you not) Avenue, a wide thoroughfare that bisects the city east to west. I have to say that, in contrast to most meals I had in China, this one was excellent – well, most of it. The courses were many, varied and microscopic, ranging from a superb Peking Duck to a quivering dish of what I strongly believe was Bisto-flavoured spit. My whole body gave an involuntary shiver as my first and only spoonful slid effortlessly down of its own accord.

'We have a 7 a.m. start in the morning, folks,' announced Harvey. 'The coach is outside. I would suggest an early night.'

I glanced at my watch – 8.35 p.m. I never went to bed that early on my honeymoon.

'Can we make our own way back, Harvey?' called Tracey and Mick, our newly-weds and 'babies' of the tour.

'And us!' called Alan and Tony.

'Us too!' came in three more voices.

I was dying to join them, but as they were the seven youngest of the party, and, on average, twenty-five years my juniors, I thought my offer might sound a little presumptuous.

'Wait a minute, wait a minute,' said Harvey, hastily raising his hands. 'How many going?' Seven arms were thrust decisively in the air. 'And exactly *where* are you going? Couriers need to know these things, you know.'

'I just think we want to have a look at downtown Peking,' explained Tony.

'*All* Peking is downtown!' replied the courier. 'It's the most downtown city you'll ever see. There's no nightlife, you know? No shops, few lights and taxis will not pick up in the street. But if you still want to go . . .' He shrugged. 'Look, I'll write down the name of the hotel in Chinese. Keep it safe, because it is a certainty that your taxi driver will speak no English. I'll see all seven of you – hopefully – at 6.30 a.m. tomorrow morning at breakfast. Have fun.'

'Eight,' cut in Mick. 'You're coming with us, aren't you Harry?'

I was on my feet before he had finished asking.

'As you're the veteran of the group, I'll make you lance-corporal,' said Harvey. 'It'll be down to you to organize their survival.'

There was something in his tone that told me he was not altogether joking.

As we waved goodbye to the bus and set off along Fuxingmen Avenue, I felt like a butch Snow White with her seven tall dwarfs. Harvey had pointed out that when we needed a taxi, we should make for the Beijing Hotel where there was a cab rank. A chill had settled on the city and we were not dressed for it; the day itself had been humid and we were all attired in either short-sleeved tops or dresses. Rubbing our arms briskly, we strode off towards town. Tracey said she understood that what shops there were could be found in Wangfujing Street. She suggested a taxi from the Beijing Hotel in case any were still open. In the absence of a better idea, that became our plan.

The day was Full Moon Day and something of a Chinese celebration, and the massive Tian An Men Square was unusually crowded. We therefore decided to use the huge subway under the square. In addition, this would provide some ten minutes' relief from the night chill. The smooth flooring of this subway is a popular place for many parents to tug a crouching child along by its outstretched arms, in the nature of a slide. There must have been some forty or fifty little trios toing and froing across the concourse. Seizing my arms, Tracey and Mick invited me to join in the festivities. As I was at least forty-five years senior to any other 'slider' this action aroused no little curiosity from the natives.

'You're not afraid of losing face then?' asked Tracey,

as I slipped back on my buttocks for the third time in as many minutes.

'It's not my face that's bothering me, luv,' I replied, rubbing my 'cheeks' vigorously.

'Probably why it's called Full Moon Day?' suggested Tony.

Some thirty minutes later, we saw the Beijing Hotel in the distance. We had all begun to realize just how tired we were and had modified our plan. We now intended to take a cab back to our hotel by way of Tracey's recommended shops in Wangfujing Street; this would also save us searching for a second cab.

'Looks like an accident outside the Beijing,' said Alan, pointing to a mass of pedestrians crowding the pavement.

'Hey! Have you noticed anything about that crowd?' asked Tony. Without waiting for a reply, he continued, 'They are all facing the *same* way! That's not an accident – it's a bloody queue for taxis! We'll be here all night!'

He was right. Not only was he right, but the acting, unpaid, elderly lance-corporal suddenly had an overwhelming desire to relinquish his rank.

Twenty minutes shirt-sleeved queueing on a chill Peking evening had done little for our composure. Although the line was just about moving, no one had tagged on behind us. Perhaps if we could pass thirty minutes or so in the warm somewhere, the queue might be even shorter on our return. I thought it worth a try. Just past an adjacent street I could see the dim yellow light of a small café.

It was time the lance-corporal made a decision. 'Why don't we adjourn to that café for a bit of local atmosphere and a beer or something? It'll give the queue a chance to shorten.'

I was a little taken aback by everyone's agreement. Still rubbing our arms, we hastened towards the gloomy light.

'Tracey!' snapped Alan suddenly, 'can you see the name of that street? That dark one there, next to the hotel.' He pointed up to the usual Chinese letters. Beneath them was an English translation – WANGFU-JING STREET.

We had been waiting in a patient line to go to a totally dark destination that was marginally closer to us than the head of the taxi queue. I congratulated myself. At least *I* had been right. Who knows? Perhaps I had a flair for this supervision game?

Okay, so my first idea worked, but unfortunately the troops were not at all impressed with my second. The café looked about the most sordid tip in the eastern hemisphere.

'Phew!' exhaled Mick, screwing up his face. 'The place stinks.'

'Don't worry about it,' I assured him. 'It's not their fault. The town's not been the same since David Niven blew up the sewers in *Fifty-five Days In Peking.*'

'Well, he missed this one,' complained Mick. 'But it not only stinks, it's so bloody gloomy. We're not going in there, surely?'

'So it's a little dark,' I said bravely. 'Come seven o'clock, everywhere's dark in China. Come on, let's give it a try.'

I could feel their reluctance as I pushed open the door. I only hoped they could not feel mine.

If it looked bad outside, it was horrendous inside. Only with great difficulty did I choke back the words 'Let's run!' The room was about twelve feet square with an earth floor and a very low ceiling. It was furnished with six greasy wooden tables and about twenty or so assorted chairs, the plaster was crumbling from the walls and a naked sixty-watt bulb hung fly-speckled from the ceiling. Back home, it would have been at least five years' work for even the most forgiving of sanitary inspectors. The three occupants, two small middle-aged men and a slightly taller younger man, could not at first hide their surprise at our entry. The older of the group seemed to gather his wits first. He circuited one of the tables with eight quickly gathered chairs and motioned for us to sit.

'Now we are here, what do we want?' asked Tony. 'He obviously can't speak English.'

'Beer is a beer in any language, surely,' I faltered.

'Ah, beer! Beer!' exclaimed our host.

'See! What did I tell you?' I said, cheering up immensely. 'Everyone knows beer.'

'Yes, but I don't want *beer*,' pointed out Tracey. 'I don't think either of us girls do. We'd like a Coke.'

'Okay,' I responded cheerfully, 'we'll ask him for a Coke. He's bound to know that.' I turned to the waiter; '. . . and four Cokes please.' I held up four fingers and he nodded wisely. The eight of us sat and began to take stock of our surroundings.

I had taken an immediate liking to the whole bunch. The newly-weds, Tracey and Mick, were two slim Mancunians in their mid-twenties. Alan and Tony had only met on the tour but had been required to share a room and were still on good terms in spite of that. The same went for the two young girls, Sue and Lynne. Last was Nadia, a fellow Londoner and, judging by the amount of times she laughed, an extremely happy girl. It was difficult to believe that each had met for the first time only three days before.

'Ah, beers!' I announced as four dark brown bottles were placed on our table, to be followed by four filthy, chipped mugs. A second member of the staff arrived with a plate and solemnly served the girls with a cucumber each; Nadia promptly dissolved. 'No! No! No!' I shouted. 'They want *Coke*. C-O-K-E. Yes? Not cucumbers!'

The host looked puzzled: 'CERK?' he asked.

I nodded vigorously. He also nodded and returned to the rear of the room. He re-emerged seconds later with four large but misshapen tomatoes. Again he served the girls with them, only this time he plopped them down on the grimy table. Nadia was now verging on hysteria.

'Look,' said Alan, 'let's cut our losses here. We'll pay him and go. The girls are obviously never going to get their Coke and I couldn't drink out of these mugs to save my life.' Without waiting for a reply he called for the bill.

'Oh, I don't know,' I protested, as I gulped down a couple of mouthfuls, whilst trying desperately to avoid touching the rim with my lips. 'It's not *that* bad.'

The now-smiling waiter approached and handed Alan, not the bill he was expecting, but a plastic menu-card that was so greasy that we could have fried bears on it.

'No! No!' Alan shouted. 'Not the *menu* – the bill! You know . . . money, money – yes?' He rubbed his thumb and finger together several times.

'Ah!' said the waiter, the light of recognition dawning on him. He held up a finger to indicate patience and shuffled to the back of the premises again. This time all three emerged and each of them had a handful of local money.

In China, there are two currencies, local and tourist. Judging by the amount of times the traveller is approached, it is pretty obvious that there is a lot of money to be made by Chinese who lay their hands on tourist notes. What a day they were having! Not only had eight foreigners appeared out of nowhere and ordered beer and cucumber, but now some of them even wanted to change their money! This reputation for inscrutability does not apply to Chinese if they think they are making money. Then, they positively chuckle.

'The only way we can get out of here,' said Alan, 'is simply to get up and go. We'll leave something for the beer and leg it.'

So that was what we did. True, we were each shown the menu card again but the hotel price that we threw in for the beer absolutely delighted the trio. They probably thought we were eccentric millionaires out on the town without coats.

Because I had drained my beer (old habits die hard) I was the last to reach the pavement. I arrived just in time to hear Tony say '. . . Well, who's going to tell him?' I groaned; what now?

'Aitch, my old son,' said Nadia cheerfully. 'You know that long taxi queue we left?'

'Er – yes.'

'Well it's now twice as long. What else d'you know?'

I looked at my watch; it was eleven o'clock. The taxis were now so infrequent that the queue looked a good two-hour wait, and by that time we would have probably frozen.

'I suppose we could *walk*,' I suggested. 'It's about seven or eight miles.'

'Without a map?' asked Tony acidly.

'Wait a minute!' I sang out excitedly. 'How about them? They could be the answer!'

I pointed to where a small group of tricycle-taxi riders

sat chatting on the pavement. There were four of these machines, with one saddle-seat for the rider and a wide seat behind him, spanning the rear wheels, for his passenger(s). *Four* tricycles . . . *eight* of us! It was fate, surely? I could feel the doubt of my compatriots, but they knew, as I did, there was little choice if we wished to return before breakfast.

Together we approached the riders. They spoke not a word of English but after studying the written note that Harvey had given Tracey, they nodded their heads and one wrote the figure twenty on his hand. We were to be finally on our way for twenty yuan a trike. The distance was obviously greater than is customary for these tricyclists so they spent a moment distributing the weight ratio. This resulted in pairing Tracey and Mick, Sue and Alan, Lynne and Tony and me and Nadia. We climbed aboard, giving cheers of encouragement to our riders, and were off down the Fuxingmen Avenue!

'It's like *Ben Hur*!' called the delighted Lynne as she egged on her rider.

All four riders entered into the spirit of the thing and a race began to develop along the wide but mainly deserted thoroughfare. We have travelled about a mile when there was a loud crack, and immediately the legs of Tracey's rider began to whir uncontrollably as the trike swerved drunkenly across the road and into the kerbside. I had not experienced a snapped chain since I was twelve years old but I recognized it instantly.

'Is it terminal?' asked Nadia, without a smile on her face for the first time that night.

'It will be if he can't link it together. Even then he will have to pedal extremely carefully,' I explained.

Although the two other machines continued, our rider

turned back to help. However, after a few moments' conversation, he left his colleague – to say nothing of our two friends – and stood straining on his pedals in what proved a vain attempt to join the two front-runners. After ten minutes or so, I began to watch him carefully, hoping that what I strongly suspected was not going to be true.

'I don't know how to tell you this, luv,' I said to Nadia, 'but this bloke's lost.'

'Bloody hell!' she exploded. 'A few minutes ago we were Ben Hur, now I feel like Orphan Annie.' She lifted her voice to the dark cold sky. 'Marooned on a chariot in a cold foreign land! – where are you now I need you, Charlton Heston?'

Typically Chinese, our rider refused to lose face and admit he was lost. He thought if he continued to pedal, we could never be really *sure* he was lost, so pedal he did – for miles and miles. I was just wondering whether I should burst into tears, when Nadia began laughing.

'So what's amusing you, kid?' I asked irritably.

'I'm just wondering what my mum would say,' she chuckled. 'Hopelessly lost in a foreign city, frozen stiff, on the back of a three-wheeled bike with a strange man, being pedalled by a sweating Chinese midget! I would guess you've just lost your lance-corporal's stripe, Aitch – wouldn't you?'

Of her list of mishaps, the one that bothered me most was the biting cold (primarily because I did not know her mother). Yet as she had rightly pointed out, it was not bothering our rider; sweat streamed from his every pore.

'I'm not sure,' said the girl thoughtfully, 'if we should wait for him to drop dead, or take it in turns to pedal so we can warm up. In the meantime, do me a favour Aitch?'

'What?'

'Give us a cuddle, I'm bloody perished!'

It seemed hours later that I suddenly recognized a junction that I knew was near our hotel. 'There! There! That street there!' I shouted excitedly.

'There! There! That street there!' obviously translates well into Chinese because our rider spun the trike into a dramatic right-hand turn. There, facing us, was the Friendship Hotel; I had never been so delighted to see anything.

'As he may not be alive tomorrow,' said the concerned Nadia, 'd'you think we should double his fee?'

'I'm not sure I'm alive right now,' I replied. 'Nevertheless, I agree. It will be my last grand gesture before I die of hypothermia. Forty yuan it *is*.'

We had assumed at that stage that because of the long detour, we were the last pair to return. It was not until breakfast that Tracey and Mick, castigating our lack of concern, pointed out that their reappearance was made some forty minutes after ours. Not only that, their rider had in fact been the owner of the whole quartet of tricycles. It was he who had negotiated – and expected – the full eighty yuan. There was almost an international incident when Mick told him, in shaking-head-and-fist language, that he wasn't getting it.

'Nothing worse than a communist entrepreneur,' complained Mick. 'They'd rob you blind.'

That day, we were to have – perhaps undergo may be a better word – our first internal flight. We were due three of these: firstly, Peking to Xian; secondly, Xian to Chungking; finally, Wuhan to Shanghai. Most internal tourist flights use military airfields, so they can shoot you for desertion should your nerve fail. Certainly, two of these flights are a little hairy, but Xian to Chungking is a real Victoria Cross job. I remember musing, whilst lost in clouds 5000 feet above the Yangtse, why it was that for a generation we in the west worried about the military threat of China, when it took them a day and a half to get a plane in the air. Unfortunately, the sheer size of the country compels the time-limited traveller to make these plane trips. One's apprehension is not lessened by the habit English-speaking Chinese have of regaling the listener with stories of the sheer inaccessibility of Chungking. 'Japanese-not-find-during-war,' they proudly proclaim. 'Not find', to a Chinese, means it was not actually flattened. They found it all right, but only on a minority of raids carried out. The reason is, the surrounding terrain acts as a cauldron and the humidity and pollution from the great city is trapped and hangs heavily throughout the region.

The 'Flying Tigers', an American fighter-plane force during the 1939–45 war, needed a base they *could* find in these mists. The problem was solved by building a landing strip on a small island in the Yangtse, plumb in the centre of town. On returning to base, they simply flew on until they found the river. Then, skimming its muddy waters, they landed on the tiny, narrow island – simple. I thought about this, then asked what happened if a pilot religiously followed the river . . . but in the wrong direction?

'Bad-luck-to-ask-such-question,' replied our guide cheerfully.

Well, I did not want to cause anyone bad luck. I just hoped air traffic control had improved a little since those days. The idea of a 747 coming in on something the size of a cricket pitch, in the middle of a foggy river between two mountains, played havoc with my bowels.

To fly with any airline is, I suppose, an act of trust. I

mean, we never actually *see* the air traffic controller; but then neither would we expect to. We assume he is in his rightful place, in front of his screen and not sending us the wrong way up the Yangtse. Now this is all very well for controllers, but what about pilots? What about that bloke who is supposed to be sitting up the front, peering through the mist like an oriental James Stewart – what about him?

Well for a start, I never saw him. After the third flight, I found this rather disquieting; unless we were flying a SAM missile, he had to be there. Yet I wondered if my lack of success in spotting him was because I was looking for the wrong image. It goes without saying that most airline pilots are smartly-dressed smoothies, who look as if they have just played the lead in an old Errol Flynn picture – but I strongly suspect that Chinese pilots are still clad in leather helmets and goggles and own long white sticks and labradors.

Another intriguing aspect of travel in China is the complete inability of airline staff to tell the time. They have a cute way around this problem – they have no clocks. In fact, clocks lose their importance after a while; disregarded, they no longer matter. This absence of clocks goes some way to explain their flight schedules and staffing levels. But if they could find a quorum, they usually took off. Marco Polo, on the other hand, kept better time.

If this account sounds too critical, then in fairness I should point out the marvellous generosity shown to all passengers. On each flight, every traveller is given a small present, for example a bag, slippers or perhaps a wallet. However, most people on a Chungking flight would settle for parachutes.

'Honey,' said an American serviceman sitting two seats away from me, to his wife. 'We must have dropped a clear thousand feet there.'

I almost told him the plane was not the only thing to have fallen. I would have probably been more assured if the illuminated sign that lit up during our plummeting had not been upside down and back to front. NO SMOKING – FASTEN SEAT BELTS does not have the same urgency when it reads:

NO SMOKING – FASTEN SEAT BELTS

After this fall, the atmosphere on the plane improved considerably. The stewardesses began to smile, and although I had never seen alcohol served on internal flights, I had the feeling we were about to get lucky. Most people soon forgot the silent promises they had just made. 'Get me out of this one God and I'll give up drink/cigarettes/grass/horses/bad language/women/men for ever – honest! (My selection was cigarettes, horses, grass and men. I figured that with all God had on His plate at that time, He wouldn't notice I wasn't giving up anything I liked.) A huge metal container was pushed up the gangway; it certainly looked like a drink container to me. Perhaps a wee celebratory one? Those who had promised to give up drink looked suitably worried, as well they might. After all, they weren't down yet.

The stewardesses began to serve thick sealed packages that made liquid noises, and they then produced straws. Expectations fell – the drinker would therefore not know texture, colour, or content. Yet, in the centre of this heavily-printed Chinese packaging, two English words clearly stood out: CONTAINS YIZHI. 'What-the-hell-is-yizhi?' quickly overtook silent prayer as dialogue. Unadventurous, I gave it a miss. I had got by so far without yizhi, and for all I knew it could be habit-forming. The upside-down reversed warning lights flashed once more; the plane ricocheted just a few times off the runway, but soon came to a halt. A sizable French contingent on board burst into instant and prolonged applause. But they always were an emotional lot.

During one of the many delays, the inevitable discussion began on Chinese safety standards. An American businessman told the group that some weeks before, he was waiting in a Chungking departure lounge for an aircraft that was three hours overdue. Suddenly, the Tannoy gave an announcement in English. This is rare, and will only usually happen in time of war, collision, or the luggage coming in on time. Overcoming his surprise, he was further intrigued to hear it was his flight being spoken of. 'Plane will not now take off . . . plane sick,' sang the metallic voice. 'New plane on way.' A further hour elapsed before the voice crackled cheerfully into life again. 'New plane, more sick than old plane,' it bubbled. 'Therefore . . . old plane . . . now fly.'

The Terracotta Army stands expectant and formidable, some thirty miles from the city walls of Xian. Of the thirty-two people in our party, it was a fair bet that the majority had come for this more than anything else. We were not disappointed. Row upon row. Hundred upon hundred. All with different expressions. All with different posture. No picture can capture it, and perhaps that is why they don't let you try. Photography is strictly forbidden. I can never resist a little smirk over this. I am possibly the most unenthusiastic photographer in the world – I am certainly the worst. A twenty-four-exposure film will last me two years and four continents. On the second week of any package tour, if I am caught taking a snap, the group usually erupts into a standing ovation, and word will probably be sent to the president. But snigger they may; when photography is banned, I like it. Everyone comes down to my level, and I find that reassuring.

Sacrilegious though the theory is, I have nagging doubts about the authenticity of those so-called 'Warriors'. The Chinese would have you believe that this army was to escort the first emperor, Qin Shi Huang, on his journey into the next world. Believe that, you'll believe anything. No, every traveller who has set foot in China over the last fifteen years will tell you exactly what these figures are; they are six thousand tourists who waited so long for their luggage they became fossilized. The fact that this army remained undiscovered for so long is no fluke. It remained undiscovered for the simple reason that it was never there in the first place. The Chinese, we know, have the largest population in the world, and no visitor could fail to be impressed by the sheer numbers of them. They are everywhere in their millions. So how come these teeming masses failed to spot six thousand warriors queueing up neatly, slap-bang in the middle of the country, until March 1974? It is no coincidence that it was not until the mid-seventies that China woke up to tourism. I believe these figures were the first bunch to arrive. Judging by their faces, they are probably Japanese.

I base this story on three facts. Firstly, the 'army' has no weapons. The Chinese explain this oversight by claiming a fire destroyed all the wooden weapons and chariots – Ha! This same fire then caused the roof of the gallery (departure lounge?) to collapse and cover the figures. I ask you!

My second fact came as a result of a purchase I made in the museum shop. It was, the curator solemnly assured me, a miniature terracotta warrior. I now believe it was a small Japanese boy, because the first time I handled it, an arm fell off. This amputation would be in keeping with someone who had been queueing since 1974.

My third and most convincing reason is pure experience. Anyone who has travelled in China *knows* these figures cannot be anything else *but* passengers waiting for their cases. They have that look about them – dead-eyed and fed-up.

With our flight for Chungking due within the hour, our coach crossed the airfield and stopped at the tumbledown building that doubled as a departure lounge. Harvey, our courier, jumped off and disappeared inside.

He returned with a thoughtful expression. 'Good and bad news, I'm afraid,' he announced. 'There is a thirty-hour flight delay and we will have to find a hotel for the night.'

A groan rose from the group. 'And the good news?' cried a voice.

Harvey rummaged in the large satchel that he always kept beside him. 'The good news is you can all have a banana.'

'Thanks a bunch,' said the dejected voice.

We could all see one great problem here; even with a well-planned itinerary, Chinese hotels were not the Ritz. In fact, some were barely doss-house standard. Therefore, thirty-four people dumped down at a moment's notice could have problems. That turned out to be a fair assumption. The hotel was *not* the Ritz; it wasn't *even* a doss-house. Oh that it had been!

Take my room, for example. On the credit side, it was spacious and roomy, with a settee, shower, TV, fridge and flowers. Unfortunately, it was too large to keep warm, the settee had broken arms and no bottom, the shower did not work, the TV had no picture, the fridge would not open – and the flowers were dead. On the debit side, windows were missing, there were no cupboards, curtains or pillows and both taps exploded on use. But worst of all, oh so much worst of all, were the stomach-turning, blancmange-pink tiles that were everywhere.

The standard did not fall at breakfast. There was one knife between three, they had run out of cups and glasses and the food had the texture of waxed grit. On the other hand, I was no longer eating and at least they served the best cup of tea in China, albeit in a crumpled second-hand plastic pot. (I had ceased eating because of stomach cramp, although I was drinking a great deal. I had purchased what I thought were six cartons of orange-juice. At first sip I realized instantly it was not orange. Asking our guide for a translation, I found out it was soya-bean milk. I can recommend it – it was delicious.)

'Okay folks,' called the sympathetic-voiced Harvey during breakfast. 'Back on the coach for another crack at that plane to Chungking.'

It was shortly after dawn as we drove across the flat Chinese landscape towards the airstrip. Already in the fields people were working: old men, young children, pregnant women and cripples, labouring singly or in families. The one thing all had in common was that they *worked*. Every back was bent.

'You know what?' murmured Frank, who at seventy-plus was our oldest companion. 'I'm rather pleased I won't be around in twenty years or so, because this country is waking up. And when she finally does, she's going to put the whole world out of work.'

He got no argument from me.

It was ironic that after such a delay, we were running short on time. The problem had been that the hotel was thirty-five miles from the airport and the road was narrow, with the occasional unpassable donkey. As we neared Xian I saw in the distance a magnificent puffing steam train running parallel to us. Soon the space between us narrowed until we were finally running neck-and-neck. Our driver was hoping to beat the train to the crossing, because in any Chinese town, once the crossing closes, it takes half an hour for normality to be resumed. It was like an old silent film, except in silent films the good guys always won – we lost.

'Don't worry,' said the unconcerned Harvey. 'The pilot has already waited thirty hours. He'll certainly wait a few minutes more. You'll be all right.'

He did. *We* were. Three hours later we were in Chungking.

I shall always remember Chungking; it is the place where couriers become honest. They can afford to, for there is nowhere else for the tourist to run. Harvey had made his customary reconnaissance of the hotel and had returned to our coach.

'I am afraid this is definitely a banana job, folks,' he confessed. 'In fact this place, plus the boat tomorrow, is worth a compensation bunch to anyone.'

He pulled out yet another great handful of the wretched things.

'Any *good* news?' asked the customary voice, 'apart from the bananas, of course.'

'There may be,' murmured Harvey thoughtfully as he rummaged deep into the satchel. 'Yes there is,' he added triumphantly, 'I haven't enough to go round.'

I suppose the classification of the place should have told us something. It was officially called a 'Guest House', meaning even the Chinese did not have the brass neck to call it a hotel. It had everything the previous hotel had, plus more wildlife than Woburn, and amazingly, it sported a reasonable-sized open-air pool. Unfortunately, every sinister, squiggling, six-legged bug east of Tibet swam happily across its surface. The rooms were poorly lit. This was no oversight. Whenever I turned my head in my bedroom, I would see just the faintest of quick movements in the shadows, but because of the gloom, I was never quite sure what it was I had just missed seeing.

Next morning at breakfast, I mentioned to Mick how tired he looked.

'Can you wonder?' he asked tersely. 'Tracey insisted on leaving the light on all night.'

'Why?' I asked.

'She said, "If it is dark, 'things' might come out of the skirting." So I just lay in bed with visions of a long line of beetles and a starter saying "Okay lads, on your marks. As soon as he puts the lights out – GO!!" '

There was one rather nice touch in my room though; in spite of the cockroaches, grasshoppers, mice and mysterious shadows, in spite of the smell from the cupboard which hinted that three people might have been walled up, in spite of the dusty red rag that hung down in lieu of curtains, there was a polythene-bagged pair of old sandals which displayed the message: 'These sandals have been disinfected for your health.'

On any tour during the football season, I ring home for the Millwall result. I was silly enough to do this in Chungking. I asked reception if I could make a call from the telephone in the foyer; the call was booked and I waited for the operator to call back. Ninety minutes later, I still waited.

'Okay, cancel,' I told the receptionist. 'I'm too tired to wait any longer.'

'Operator-put-call-through-to-room-sir,' he offered.

'Great!' I immediately ran up six flights to my room – no telephone.

Minutes later I was back at reception. 'Look!' I snapped angrily, 'I don't *have* a telephone in my room!'

''S okay-sir. Operator-now-say . . . "No-call-sir".' He smiled politely.

I groaned wearily and trudging back up the stairs, made tracks for bed. Five minutes later, I was under a spitting shower when the whole building was plunged into power-cut darkness. This was at the same instant that someone knocked loudly on my door and announced – 'Quick-sir. London-on-phone-for-you-sir. Downstairs-now-sir.'

To be fair, the tour operator had warned of power-cuts in their brochure and had suggested a torch be packed. That was exactly what I did – pack a torch. Trouble was, I had packed it in my suitcase and until five minutes previous, I had not seen that particular item for close on three days. Running towel-clad and dripping-wet down six flights of dark stairs, in a dubious Chungking Guest House, to be told that your team has just been stuffed by Crystal Palace, could make a soccer hooligan of Moses.

This needless aggravation did little for a good night's

sleep, yet a good night's sleep would have been a gilt-edged investment in view of what lay ahead. We assembled in the foyer at 5.45 a.m. and swopped 'room' stories. No one had lost a limb or been devoured during the night, so we were correct in complement. Not only that, but having been briefly reunited with our cases, we even appeared a little more presentable. The coach rumbled its way to the riverside docks and the reason for this reunion with our baggage became instantly apparent. Our steamer was moored at the bottom of some two hundred wet, crumbling, unlit rubbish-strewn steps. It was still dark, with the only light filtering up from the docked steamer.

'Careful here,' called Harvey, cheerfully. 'Had a bloke last time who fell and broke his leg. Had to shoot him, I'm afraid.'

We may not have believed the story but we well believed the message.

Minutes later, we struggled on to the boat. It was a large, flat, four-decked wedding-cake-shaped vessel, typical of the type that ply between the Yangtse's towns and cities. On Harvey's instructions, we assembled in the small forward lounge for 'a discussion'.

'Of the thirty-four of us,' he began, 'seven pairs will be in second class, which is a primitive but fairly adequate cabin, and the remainder will be in third class. This is also a cabin but three times larger and quite disgusting. However, even that is better than fourth class, which is evil. Chinese, by the way, do not have first class.'

'How disgusting is "disgusting"?' came the question.

'Well, the unlucky eighteen, plus Rose Li and myself, will be in the eight-berth cabins along with the locals. There are no washing facilities and you'll doubtless find the spitting a little nauseating. If you think that's bad, wait till you see the communal loos – they are unbelievable.' There was a look of uncertainty all round but no one spoke, so Harvey continued. 'Best way is to draw lots. I would further suggest that those lucky enough to draw a cabin allow the unfortunates access to their washbasins. Oh, and one more thing. One of the lavatories is broken, so there are only two for the forward part of the boat. I do like to get the bad news over and done with, don't you?'

I consider I am a lucky person but I was mighty relieved to be amongst the 'winners'. Needless to say, the losers hastened quickly along to third class, just 'to see'. Harvey had not exaggerated – it was horrendous. The boat's communal lavatories were also something of a novelty. They consisted of a hole in the floor, a hose pipe and a recess for feet. There was no lock, light, or loo paper. In addition, the doors had a mind of their own; they would not open when you wished to enter, or close once you were inside. With the recess for feet being a feature, the only lavatorial comfort the Chinese seemed to expect was dry feet. For the first time on the tour I was delighted to be constipated.

Harvey then handed everyone a sheet and a large towel. 'You'll need these; firstly because the bedding may be a little suspect, and secondly because tomorrow night we are on a sleeper-train, which is slightly inferior to the boat.'

'Why the towel?' he was asked.

'The towel you can use as a blanket. You won't need anything heavier, it's far too warm . . . banana, anyone?'

A wartime spirit soon pervaded our group. Facilities were offered by the fortunate fourteen, including sleeping space should anyone wish to sleep on the floor. Soon, the tiny two-berth cabins were crowded with cases and, a few hours later, strip-washers. Privacy and modesty vanished and there seemed a permanent queue for the two lavatories. I prayed my constipation would last one more day.

The boat docked to take on and discharge passengers at two small Yangtse towns, each stop taking twenty minutes or so. Many were turned back at the jetty but no one complained; they just stood passively and awaited the next boat, whenever that was. We watched in admiration as a slightly-built man, carrying a washing machine on his back, trotted up the 200 stairs from the riverside. His knees faltered on the last dozen or so steps but he made it! We burst into instant applause. These towns were very similar; perched on high cliffs, they could only be reached from the river by these well-used and treacherous steps.

Harvey had not lied over the fourth-class areas, they were packed and stinking. I could not suppress a guilty feeling as I watched a breast-feeding mother, cross-legged on cardboard, in a packed, humid gangway. The sweat poured from the gulping offspring. People were crammed everywhere; in every recess, every doorway, every stair. There were bags, packages and bundles, fruit, vegetables and animals. Babies cried, old men slept and almost everyone spat.

We docked for the night at Wanzian, and again dark stone steps led up to the town. Some of us climbed them to discover a very busy night market, with the amazing hours of 7 p.m.–5 a.m.! The stalls sold everything from beans and beads to cats and carpets. The trader most sought after by our bunch was a little lad selling jasmine-flowered necklaces. Hoping they would be an antidote to certain aquatic aromas, I bought three. They failed miserably.

Our litle group appeared something of a novelty to the townspeople. If we stopped to look at anything, a crowd would form to look at us. I soon realized that nothing delighted Chinese parents more than our speaking to their children. It mattered not a bit that no one had a clue what anyone was saying; attention was paid and that sufficed. This was no hardship anyway, for the toddlers were all marvellous. They wore no napkins or diapers, they simply had large slits in the backs of their trousers. I suppose this cuts down on washing, but there must be a few million cold bums in the winter.

Returning to the boat, I found I could barely enter my cabin. It was clustered with space-devouring cases and strip-washing females, so I gallantly retired to the lounge. The traffic in and out of my cabin eased, and together with other 'draw-winners', I took up a seat in the lounge that gave a clear view along the badly-lit gangway of our respective cabin doors. As soon as the last of the refugees had used our facilities for the night, we could all retire, if not to bed, then to whatever comfortable corner we could call our own until dawn. My last customer was Harvey, who always carried the tour's vital documents in a leather pouch that rarely left his side; because of his impending ablutions, he had tied it to his waist. However, it had swung round to hang sporran-like over his groin. The poor light plus his pale shirt and trousers made it appear, certainly to my tired eyes, as if he was clad in nothing but an extremely large, ill-fitting, leather jockstrap.

'Why is Harvey only wearing a brown leather jockstrap?' I asked, hoping to lighten the stupor that had crept over my compatriots. No one bothered to show interest.

A few minutes later, Harvey reappeared clutching his personal toilet roll (an essential item for a China tour) and obviously heading for the lavatory.

'He's now got a jock-strap *and* a toilet-roll,' I persisted.

Tracey raised a particularly weary head. 'Just where does one wear a toilet roll?' she asked, without bothering to open her eyes.

'You slide it over your banana, you dozy cow,' replied Mick from deep in an armchair.

Nadia chuckled in her sleep.

The toing and froing finally ended as Tracey, Mick, Alan and myself wedged ourselves into the tiny room. The heat was stifling as the cabin's fan fought a losing and noisy battle. I thought it might keep me awake but I discovered next morning that I was probably the only member of our whole group who had slept. I hadn't the courage to tell anyone that not only had I slept, but I had slept particularly well. Complaints abounded at breakfast, understandably really; but I couldn't complain. The cost of the tour had certainly been expensive, but I still had visions of the poor breast-feeding woman on a cardboard mat.

Shortly after breakfast, excitement began to spread amongst the group. One more river bend, then we would reach what, together with the Terracotta Army, we had travelled thousands of miles to see – the first of the three incredible Yangtse river gorges; a full hundred and twenty miles of breathtaking scenery. First was the magnificent Qutang Gorge. No pictures could have prepared us for its majesty. Then came the Wu Gorge, which for thirty miles cuts through the Wushan mountains like a deep winding corridor of paintings. Finally came the Xiling Gorge, which, although I found it unpronounceable, is mesmeric with its shoals, currents and mysterious whirlpools. The many hidden creeks and inlets could well have provided haven for a score of pirate junks; but what would they seek to capture? Not *this* steamer for sure.

I found it interesting that throughout the gorges the British stood, whilst the Germans sat. They sat because, like the 'towels-on-deckchairs' syndrome, they had arisen about four in the morning to deposit coats and stormsuits on the few available seats. I have promised myself that one holiday, I am going to rise at 3 a.m. and chuck every article of kraut clothing in the sea. Perhaps fate resented these dark thoughts, because later, whilst chancing a shower from a dripping warm-water pipe, my clothes fell in the drain.

At the east end of the gorges is the city of Yichang, with a truly gigantic dam and lock system. Because of the river traffic, the lock is very congested as it rises and falls to its different levels. Alongside us in the lock, so close that we touched fingers with its passengers, was a luxury steamer full of Americans – and I do mean *luxury*! It was palatial. Nadia asked Harvey if we could receive food parcels or use their lavatories. Mick suggested a boarding-party.

'Come on Harry!' he enthused. 'You're a Millwall fan. Let's be real Brits. Why don't we piss up their boat and sling beer cans around?'

We later docked, collected our cases and moved happily to the gangway for disembarkation. One small light bulb, on an otherwise dark dockside, revealed a distressing sight. Hundreds of people were massed in the dark, each trying to clamber aboard, like scared survivors from a plague city. Scuffles had broken out, and because of the confusion at the foot of the ramp, we were unable to disembark. There appeared to be no system; passengers crowding the gangways to leave had been met by four times as many trying to board, and for a while there was impasse. Soon, however, uniformed officials arrived and pounded a path through the waiting humanity, along which we filed sheepishly to our coach.

We were approaching the last lap of our stay in China, an overnight train to our last three days in Shanghai. Harvey's warning about the sleeper had caused a little apprehension amongst some, but I now had a whole new problem – my constipation had gone, but it had been replaced by something that made me yearn nostalgically for its quick return. Chinese trains have two classes, 'soft' and 'hard'. At least this journey did not necessitate a 'lucky draw', for there were thirty-two soft-class vacancies and thirty-two tourists. Professionals to the end, Harvey and the luckless Rose took up their positions in the hard.

Our sleeping accommodation was four bunks in a tiny compartment, with two either side at floor level and two similarly aligned at eye level. The gangway between was barely sufficient to allow one person to dress. Or two, if they were four years old and small for their age. It had been decided that the ladies should have the bottom bunks, and the men, the tops. The big problem for us all was the heat – we could have boiled chickens. I tried reading, but with no fan, the trickles of sweat kept running in my eyes. With all four of us experiencing the same problem, the light was turned out and we tried to sleep. Being out of sight in the top bunk, I shed everything and, surprisingly, soon dozed off.

I awoke two hours later, convinced I was dead. I did

not believe anyone could be so cold and survive. The heating had completely reversed, and those rivulets of sweat were now minute glaciers that cut across my skin like arctic streams. In addition, I needed the toilet – oh how I needed the toilet! Shivering, I looked for the track-suit in which I had spent most of the tour. I saw it instantly; it had fallen to the floor, together with my underpants and shirt. All that I had at that moment was hypothermia (and a pair of socks). I had no time to stand on ceremony, but swinging quickly down, I could see a problem. Supposing young Nadia beneath was not asleep?

Now I do not consider myself over-modest, but I can well understand that a loose-bowelled, fifty-eight-year-old retired copper, clad in only his socks, would not necessarily be the Rambo-type answer to the maiden's dream. Above all girl, I thought, don't scream, although what little I had learned about her on the tour indicated that she would be more inclined to dissolve into great gales of laughter. In the event, she did neither.

I made three of those trips during that night, although on the last two I was at least more sensibly attired. It was next morning that I discovered that what I had taken to be a well-padded soft mattress was in fact a side-zipped duvet. Almost everyone else in our party had slipped inside theirs, and once the heat subsided, slept like tops.

Shanghai was easily the most commercial town we had seen on our trip. We had excursions to theatre, circus, factories, schools and markets: yet just a few words at a brief talk, in a lecture-room of a state-commune, explained more about China than any book, guide or propaganda could ever do. We had undertaken a tour of this vast commune, and its leader, via an interpreter, volunteered to answer any questions put to him. There were a few predictable ones, then a lady from our group arose.

'Let us say, someone comes to work for you and after three months, they decide they don't like it. What then?'

The interpreter translated and it was obvious the leader was genuinely puzzled. He then seemed to make a short reply.

'Leader says he is sorry but does not understand question. Please repeat.'

The woman repeated her question but this time broke it down into parts.

'Let us say, I come to work for you . . . yes?'

The interpreter dutifully explained and the leader nodded his head in understanding.

'I work for you for, say, three months . . . yes?'

The same ritual took place.

'Then after three months, I say to you, "I don't like it." What then?'

Once more the interpreter conveyed the message. This time the leader erupted into great fat chuckles and sang out a few words in reply.

'Leader says,' explained the interpreter, 'no such reason.'

As the holiday grew to a close, it was inevitable that we should ask each other our impressions. The overriding one was the complete friendliness of the people, and of course, without exception, we all adored the children. Many parts of the trip were particularly breathtaking – other parts were breathtaking but for the wrong reasons. To spend two weeks in China is not even to scratch the surface, and yet it is fascinating; the place will probably change the attitude of western travellers more than anything they have experienced before. All those little luxuries that we in the west take for granted, such as food, drink, sleep and hygiene, are discovered to be surprisingly dispensable.

The one thing the traveller will find *in*dispensable, however (unless the plan is for a solo run along the Great Wall), is a good guide. Good guides are those who do not scream, head-bang or chuck bananas about until at least eight days into the tour. They are not needed to point out the visually obvious, i.e. the Warriors, the Wall or the river gorges. No, their role in China is more that of a coach preparing the team for that vital game.

His role therefore, is to:

(1) Convince you that no matter what lies in wait for you, you *can* cope.
(2) Enable you to return home and *not* sue your tour company.
(3) Actually cause you to say – 'You know, I may even go *back* there one day.'

Like I say, our guide was good; not brilliant, just good. After all, I did cope – well, just about. I did not sue – well, not quite. As for going back – well, two out of three's not bad.

There was a footnote to this trip. Twenty minutes out of Shanghai to Hong Kong, I placed my cardigan in the locker above my head, lay back in my seat and closed my eyes. I was immediately aware of a light tap on my right wrist. I opened my eyes to see Nadia leaning across the gangway.

'Sorry to disturb you, Aitch,' she said, 'but you won't be taking anything else off, will you? Because you don't half look silly in just your socks.'

Hot Pies in Hong Kong

Hong Kong was going to be a 7th Cavalry job for me, or so I hoped. It had been four days since I had eaten, but as we prepared to leave Shanghai I began to feel my appetite return. My plan therefore, was for a sumptuous meal on the island, accompanied by a decent bottle of wine. The thought had me drooling, but temptation almost ruined this plan on the two-hour flight to the territory. Awkward to the end, Chinese internal airlines did not give us the customary present – instead they served up two superb cheese sandwiches. Now I fully realize that 'superb' is not an adjective normally used to describe cheese sandwiches of any ilk, least of all Chinese and served up in plastic airline wrappings. But a four-day abstention, plus my life-long adoration of the stuff, made refusal particularly hard.

Eventually, Hong Kong lay beneath us; well – just. I say 'just' because one gets the feeling on the approaches to the airport that the whole city is pushing up out of the ground so hard and so high, that soon it will no longer be *beneath* anything. It will simply tower up and up until planes will not be able to fly over it at any height. This feeling is not helped by the runway, which is not actually on the island at all but on the mainland side in Kowloon. In fact, it is almost true to say that it isn't even in Kowloon, because it sticks out into the sea so far that passengers tend to think they should have travelled by boat. If ever they need to lengthen the runway, all they will need to do is to whack on a couple of dozen Chinese junks and no one will know the difference.

The Lee Gardens hotel has two great advantages going for it. Firstly, it is a splendid hotel and secondly, and far more importantly, particularly for our two Mancunians, it is adjacent to a hot meat-pie shop. One needs to spend two weeks feasting on the rice and sea cucumbers of China to realize that a good hot meat-pie is truly one of the great dishes of the world. If I had been tempted by the sight of a Chinese cheese sandwich, then the smell of a hot meat-pie drove me to distraction. It says a great deal for my character that my resolution held – although I must confess, both Mick and Tracey broke me off a corner.

We had been allocated our rooms, and chattered excitedly as we left the elevator and searched for the relevant numbers. I had been in my room but a few seconds when I heard a loud scream. It was so close, it had to be one of our party. Running to the door, I emerged into the corridor at the same time as seven or eight other members of our group. The only door not opened in the immediate proximity was the one next to mine.

'I think it's Nadia,' said Lynne anxiously, as she moved towards that very door.

I pounded heavily upon it and virtually the whole group began to call through the crack in unison. The door was opened so quickly we practically fell into the room. A bemused Nadia stood open-mouthed before us.

'What's the matter, kid?' I asked worriedly. 'Why the scream?'

'Scream?' she echoed, looking in puzzlement from one

to another. 'I didn't scre – Oh!' For a moment she clamped both hands quickly to her mouth. 'I s'pose I did,' she eventually agreed. 'I'm ever so sorry Aitch; you see, it's the bathroom.'

'The *bathroom*? What on earth have you got in the bathroom that caused you to scream like that?'

She smiled sheepishly. 'A bath.'

'A what!!'

'A bath. I've not had a bathroom that's actually had a *bath* with *hot* water in it since we left Peking. I suppose I was so delighted, I just screamed. I don't even remember doing it.' She hunched her shoulders and gave an impish grin; 'Smashin' though, ain't it?'

As alarmed as we had been about the girl's scream, she was certainly right about the bathroom. A bath, hot water and our suitcases! What else was there in the world? After half an hour, if I had not told myself there was no point in travelling six thousand miles to lie in a bath, I would be there still.

With the exception of our return flight to Gatwick, the organized side of our holiday was finished. We were free at last! Most decided to shop – even me. The two things I can do really badly are shopping and singing – the casual listener would probably say there is little difference. But in Hong Kong, even *I* can shop – and what is more, I almost enjoyed it! Within minutes I had bought an outfit for my grandson, that to this day my daughter does not believe I was capable of purchasing.

'Not you dad – not you. You couldn't have bought that. You can't even buy your own socks, so how come you can rig out a three-year-old boy, from six thousand miles away?'

Actually, there was a grain of truth in this; about the

socks, I mean. In addition to my grandson's outfit, I certainly bought myself some socks. Sadly, I got rather carried away, primarily because I did not realize they were in 'six-packs'. Thirty-six pairs of white socks are of limited use to a fifty-eight year old, especially when his only remaining sport is swimming.

With the shopping over, I could concentrate on the main event of the day. My dinner! Not everyone returned to the hotel for the evening meal; some had friends to meet, others tried outside restaurants. So only six or seven of us sat down at 7.30 p.m. in one of the several restaurants that can be found in the Lee Gardens. It took me just seconds to choose. I would start with a Mackeson, then French onion soup, then a real thick steak with jacket potatoes *and* french fries, accompanied by a large side-salad. In addition, there were two buttered rolls and a bottle of St Emilion.

I am sure the crusty rolls were as delicious as any I have eaten; equally so the Mackeson and the onion soup. As for the rest, I will never know – it was all I could do to even look at it. Abstention for at least four days had simply ensured that two buttered rolls, a bottle of Mackeson and a bowl of French onion soup was all that the returning Chinese traveller would need. I was, in simple terms, full-up! I wasn't even hungry enough to steal my own chips! As I could not bear to see everyone else knocking back a dinner that I had lain awake for four nights planning, I donated them my wine and strolled out into the warm night air.

I suppose the main purpose of my stroll was to sulk. Yet sulk or not, I still returned with four sports shirts, two long-sleeved shirts, one cardigan and a tracksuit. The four sports shirts I purchased after midnight from easily the shiftiest-looking bandit I had seen since leaving England. How compulsive shoppers ever manage to leave Hong Kong I will never understand. Perhaps I should have stayed out buying clothes, because going to bed did not turn out to be a very good idea. On at least four occasions during the night my stomach convinced me I had been shot, and I thanked my lucky stars for a well-equipped bathroom.

Next morning was to be our last before returning home. Breakfast looked sumptuous, and it was maddening to settle for one slice of toast and marmalade, instead of three fried eggs and two of everything else. Most people intended to make the most of this final day and made an early start, with maps, time-tables and comfortable shoes. My own choice was the ferry to Kowloon and a half-day exploration of various points of interest on the mainland. To this effect, and to make the most of the time, I had studied the route on a well-marked map. I must confess I am not normally this efficient, it was simply that lack of time left bred a compulsion.

Travel in Hong Kong and the territories is relatively inexpensive. For the equivalent of an English pound, I was able to take a taxi to the ferry, some two to three miles away, and first class on the ferry to Kowloon was only about six pence. On the ferry I met Sue and Lynne, who were impressed with my planned itinerary and asked if they could accompany me. Gallant to the end and pleased to impress, I concurred. The ferry deposits its customers neatly alongside a huge bus terminal, from which many routes fan out to all parts of the territory, and the service appeared good. I took my bearings, put my hand in my trouser pocket and pulled out the map; which of the waiting buses we would select depended upon our chosen destination. I had magnanimously decided that the girls should have the choice, and they waited expectantly as I unfolded the map.

At first glance, I was a little surprised to see that the South China Sea was missing. An island with no sea? On closer inspection, the sea was not shown because I was studying a map of Chungking. As that particular city is located 750 miles inland, the absence of a sea was probably not altogether strange. If this was a map of Chungking, where was the map of Kowloon? It was, of course, exactly where I had left it – in my suitcase, back at the hotel. I had picked up the wrong bloody map! We never had this trouble before we had such easy access to our cases. There was a moral there somewhere.

Admiration of my efficiency had rapidly faded from the eyes of my two young companions. What now? Time was so limited. We might have known where we were, but we certainly did not know where to go.

'Look,' I said, as I attempted a salvage job. 'Why don't we get on the first bus to leave here and stay on it right to the end of the route? We won't stray too far from its terminus. In that way, we will know on what bus and at what time to return. It'll be like a little adventure, won't it?'

I sensed they were not impressed. However, in the absence of a more constructive idea, that was what we did. I remember hoping against hope, as the bus chugged along, that some exotic location would hove into view, but no such apparition appeared. I have not the faintest idea where we went, but it was as boring as Barnsley. The route did not even follow a main road. It simply meandered and squiggled its way through the Kowloon suburbs before coming to a final halt at a small, innocuous and rather untidy park.

'What now?' asked Sue.

I shrugged helplessly; I had lost it and I knew it. 'Perhaps we could go for a stroll and then . . . er . . . and then . . .'

'Go back?' she suggested.

'Go back,' I agreed. 'Look, I'm sorry kids but I'm afraid it's now too late to attempt anything else.'

They took it well and soon began to chatter cheerfully, even to me.

The park included a few tennis courts and two football pitches, all of which were in use. We spread ourselves on the grass between the two pitches and whilst the girls sunbathed, I watched both games and girls in turn. To add variety and prevent us from dozing, four-engined jets would roar low overhead every few minutes. We were also on the airstrip flight-path! The composition of all four football sides appeared to be Hong Kong Chinese; the only thing I learned was that Chinese footballers greet linesmen's decisions with the same disbelief as their British counterparts. This was hardly a stunning revelation and certainly not worth the trip to discover. In spite of my planning, in spite of the expense, I found myself, on a Sunday morning, doing exactly the same thing in Kowloon for fifteen hundred quid that I could have done for free on Hackney Marshes.

We had actually begun to laugh about it on our return; that is until we rejoined the rest of our group back at the hotel. 'What have you been doing with yourself this morning?' seemed to be the general question. I could scarcely believe that so many people could do so many different things in one place. Cable-cars, boat trips, scenic walks, markets and beaches, were just a few.

'So what did you do with yourself, Aitch?' asked Nadia.

'Er . . . Lynne, Sue and myself . . . er . . . went for a bus-ride . . . over in Kowloon.'

'Yes, but exactly *whereabouts* did you go?' she persisted. 'Somewhere nice?'

'Well, we went to a park actually. It was . . . er . . . quite pretty really . . . and . . . I . . . er . . . watched a football match . . . and Sue and Lynne – ' Suddenly I could tell by her face that she had already spoken to the girls and was just winding me up.

'. . . Lay on the grass and listened to the airplanes?' she inserted. 'And I bet you didn't half feel a prat!'

'Yes,' I agreed, 'I think that's a pretty fair assumption. I'll go along with that.'

By mid-afternoon we had all vacated our rooms. Harvey had managed to secure the continuing use of one double-room where we could change and freshen up prior to departure at 6.30 p.m. Those who were travelling on to such places as Australia and New Zealand said their farewells, and the rest of us adjourned to the bar-lounge. A Chinese maid discreetly approached and enquired if someone had left a small blue jewel-case on the glass shelf of the courtesy bathroom. No one admitted to such carelessness and fears were expressed that it could perhaps belong to one of those who were, even then, on their way to Sydney. At least, this denial persisted until she showed it. An increasingly red-faced Scot then explained that far from being a jewel-case, it was the container that housed his spare false teeth. 'There have been occasions though,' he explained, 'when they have been of far more use to me than Crown jewels could ever be.'

This exchange seemed to trigger off horror stories about various hotel rooms that had been experienced (although I did notice no one mentioned Chungking). Harvey then pointed out the difficulties that can arise over single rooms, on a crowded, constantly changing tour. 'Sometimes,' he said, 'particularly when the tour has been delayed late at night, couriers do not always study their lists as closely as they might.' He then described a tour he had covered the previous year. On arrival at the hotel, rooms had been limited, and a certain amount of doubling-up had therefore to be done. This seemed to work okay and the same coupling took place for the next four nights in another three towns. It was well into the fifth day when a shy, mousey, fiftyish 'Miss' approached him.

'I did realize when I booked,' she said, 'that accommodation could be scarce and that I might have to share. Now I didn't mind it for *one* night. But it has been four days now, and Mr Cornelius snores dreadfully.'

Eventually the coach arrived and within the hour we had joined the long queue at the check-in. This tends to be the time when I ease my brain into neutral and just shuffle along to the desk. I was about three places from actually checking in, when I was aware of a heavy foreign accent jabbering away close by. At this time the queue moved once more and again the same voice seemed to repeat its message. Still I paid no attention. Suddenly a tap on my left arm indicated that whatever the communication was, it was directed at me. I turned, to come face-to-face with two tall German lads aged about twenty. With some vigorous sign language and my fortuitous ability to swear and count up to ten in their language, I was able to decipher their problem. It was a pretty acute one. Their flight was due to leave Hong Kong at 9.20 p.m. and the terminal hall clock showed 9.17 p.m. They were simply asking to swop places in the queue.

My instinctive reaction was to say 'Of course!' then thrust them forward and take their place at the rear of the line. This noble gesture was momentarily stifled by my vindictive wish to enquire as to their personal viewpoint concerning the placing of towels on deckchairs; or even worse, coats on boats. However, in spite of Hitler ruining my childhood, I still rose above all racial prejudice and quickly took their place at the rear of the queue, considering I had now done my bit for Anglo-German relations. It was with a clear conscience therefore, that I crossed my fingers and hoped they still missed their plane.

This reluctant gesture left me with a rather annoying consequence. Separated from the main body of my fellow-travellers, I then had to spend the sixteen-hour return flight with a different group. Oh well, I knew no one going out, so I was sure I could cope going back.

I suppose I should have recognized the type when he first sat down – he chatted a lot and was ultra-friendly. Before the 'seat belt' sign came up, I had already heard more than enough about his hobby, photography. The irony of it did not escape me for a moment; the worst photographer in the world, sitting next to a compulsive snapper! I gritted my teeth and blamed the Germans.

One day, I am going to take a flight that either shows a film I have not already seen, or even more unusual, one that I can actually watch without paralysis of the neck. My choice was simple: to risk spondylitis and stick with the film, or gamble with my sanity for one and a half continents whilst I studied his rotten snaps. I then had an inspired thought; I would tell him I had misplaced my spectacles. It is true I would then be unable to read, but this was a small price to pay for such a reprieve. What a mistake! Of my own free will, I had given him a captive audience with no distractions.

'You won't need reading specs for these,' he announced confidently. 'Look at the clarity – a blind man could see 'em,' he enthused, as he passed over a wad of assorted Sino-snaps. Keeping up a non-stop banter, he told me he had lived in New Zealand since 1961 and this was to be his second return to England since that date. 'Of course, I'm an Arsenal supporter through and through,' he confided. He then gave a deep sigh. 'But the game's not what it was though, is it? If you want my opinion, it's gone to the dogs.'

Even making every allowance for the fact that he was an *Arsenal* supporter, this still did not fully explain such a cretinous observation from someone who had seen nothing of the game for the best part of thirty years.

'Why do you say that?' I asked, suddenly seeing an alternative to his tedious photographs.

'Well,' he said, shaking his head sadly. 'I went back in 1982 and I did not recognize one player. All gone, you see: Kelsey, Eastham, Armstrong. No wonder the game's in such a state. It's down to lack of continuity in my book, mate.'

'All gone'? The man was an idiot. What on earth was he on about? Jack Kelsey would be fifty now if he was a day! I groaned at my misfortune and yearned nostalgically for a well-wrapped silent Ethiopian I once knew.

Dawn broke just prior to our crossing of the English coast. As the aircraft descended towards Gatwick, the clouds parted and I took a sleepy stare from the window.

I could not believe what I was seeing. We had been gone a little over two weeks and within that time Sussex had fallen down. Had the 'bomb' gone off at last?

'We had a storm two days ago,' explained the captain over the intercom. 'Some say a hurricane. Anyway, whatever it was, it decimated our trees. Those of you travelling home by train may well experience some problems. There are now more trees on railway lines than there are in some forests.'

I was soon to realize that 'some problems' as defined by an airline captain is comparable to 'some discomfort' as defined by a surgeon – twin pinnacles of understatement.

I said a dozen brief, embarrassed goodbyes, and then made for the railway station. There is always something about these holiday partings that makes me feel so damn guilty; it is as if I have used people for two whole weeks and then cast them aside. I really do want to keep in touch with most, yet deep down, I know I will never see them again. Oh, we'll doubtless exchange addresses and swear to look each other up. For the next two years we may even swop Christmas cards, but unless they appear on our holiday snaps, we will never see their faces again. (As someone who decapitates most people in every photograph I have ever taken, I am denied even that tenuous connection.) Had it only been fifteen days since the start of the trip? What with the devastation and my alarming loss of weight, I felt I had returned from the war.

Every platform was packed. Staff had no idea when, where, or if, any train was running. There was nothing to do but settle down for a very long wait. I sat on my suitcase and stared blankly at the empty rails. I was suddenly aware of a familiar voice whispering from over my shoulder. It was a voice that had almost haunted me for two whole weeks and one that I thought I would never hear again. It was young Nadia.

'Listen, Aitch,' she breathed confidentially, 'there are a couple of geezers outside with bikes . . . interested?'

'Sod off!'

New York, New York

'I don't believe it! You are telling me, you're spending fifteen days in America and less than two of them in New York? How can you possibly spend so little time here? It takes longer than that to cross Second Avenue!'

I had telephoned Bob Woolley from Philadelphia to confirm the time of my arrival in New York. Bob, who had never experienced the hustle and bustle of a fifteen-day package-tour, had no idea that a two-day stay anywhere almost constituted permanency. In fact, if you stay anywhere over three days, tour companies will issue naturalization papers.

'Look Bob,' I explained. 'If I can do three hundred miles of the Nile before elevenses and the Great Wall of China between lunch and tea, New York will be a doddle.'

'You did *that* in one day?' Even at our inter-state distance, I could hear the impression I had made.

'No, you berk!' I clarified. 'I am simply saying, that grass does not grow under your feet when you are package-touring. There just isn't sufficient time. With a reasonable bus and a good tour manager, we'd have won the West for your lot, two hundred years before you did.'

'So where do I meet you?' he asked, in a tone I suspected he reserved for idiots.

'Well, we're leaving Philadelphia in a few minutes and when we arrive in New York we'll be staying at the Lexington on East Forty-eighth Street. So how about the hotel foyer at 7 p.m.?'

'Okay,' he agreed. 'I'm fetching a ladyfriend, plus a guy who has asked to meet you. I'll tell him to be in the foyer at that time. See you around seven.'

On the face of it, it had been a fairly routine conversation. The problem was I had not seen Bob for thirty-two years! In 1956, we worked together on the same shift for a few months. We had also played a little football together, but soon after that he left for Bermuda and disappeared from my life. Well perhaps not *quite* disappeared, because three months earlier, and completely out of the blue, he had sent me a letter.

'So we're meeting three people in a large, no doubt crowded, hotel foyer,' said Joan, 'two of whom you don't know from Adam, and the third you haven't seen for thirty-two years?'

I knew what was coming. 'That's about the size of it . . . yes,' I answered, as nonchalantly as I could.

'But you never remember *anyone* after a two-day absence. I swear it's only the fact that we have the same surname that you know who *I* am. If Bob doesn't recognize you as soon as he walks in that door, we'll still be in that foyer at Christmas. You don't remember anyone and you know it!'

'Now don't be silly, of course we won't still be there at Christmas. We've got to do Canada by Friday afternoon . . . and in any case, you haven't enough boiled sweets.'

We had arrived in Philadelphia from Washington on a public holiday. This fact had caused the pair of us some amusement. We had both remembered a quote from W.

C. Fields, the old-time actor, comedian and drunk, who said: 'I once went to Philadelphia but it was shut.' Although, until that moment, we had never been to the place, I knew exactly what he meant. As an evacuee child in Norfolk during the war, I had felt the same about the whole county. I loved it very much but after two and three quarter years there, I was still waiting for it to open.

As our bus arrived in the town, we had been joined by an enthusiastic young guide. 'Of course,' he said disappointedly, 'this is not a good day to be visiting our beautiful city. You see, it's Labor Day and you will find that most places are closed.' We turned to each other with a knowing smile. It appeared the old inebriate had been right after all.

Leaving behind the closed doors of Philadelphia, we soon covered the hundred or so miles to New York. This city must surely be the one place in all the world where every cinemagoer feels he has been before. Both Joan and I served a thirty-year apprenticeship in a thousand palaces and flea-pits as we saw everything from *King Kong* to *West Side Story*.

Emerging into Manhattan from the Lincoln tunnel, we were almost disappointed not to see Gene Kelly and Dan Dailey dancing up the street with dustbin lids on their feet, and time and again this feeling was to repeat itself. As our bus threaded its way through the city towards our hotel, there was a flurry of interest as the Empire State Building peaked into view. I knew instantly that something was lacking, but could not readily think what it could be.

'Where's the ape?' asked Joan in a reverential whisper. Of course! Kong should be smoothly climbing the outside of the structure with one hand, whilst gently caressing the scantily-clad, virginal Fay Wray with the other. What sort of let-down was this? No Gene Kelly and no gorilla! 'I'll tell you what,' she continued ruefully. 'Unless I hear someone singing *Maria* from a fire-escape balcony, I'm going home.'

She was right. For us, New York wasn't a city at all. It was a thousand film sets.

The hotel was situated nicely central and a few minutes after seven o'clock Joan and I took up our positions in the foyer. There was a persistent stream of people toing and froing towards reception, and some half-dozen others scattered aimlessly around. Our presence increased their total to eight. As we watched and waited, I wondered just who these people were. It struck me that I never have been in a large metropolitan hotel and not seen them. Is it all they do? I had visions of them wandering from one hotel foyer to another like well-dressed bag-people, always on the move but never actually going anywhere.

'Well,' Joan said. 'Which one is it?'

I shook my head thoughtfully. 'Bob is obviously not here yet because he's fetching a ladyfriend and everyone here is on their own.'

'I know. So how about this male friend. What did Bob say his name is?'

'He didn't.'

'You mean you are meeting a complete stranger in a foreign hotel and you didn't ask his name?'

'Er . . . well, yes, but . . .' I looked anxiously round for a suitable subject '. . . I'm fairly sure it's that bloke by the door.'

'But he's Greek.'

'So he's Greek!' I felt the tables were turning. 'Greeks

walk and talk, you know. Some have actually been known to converse, in fact most of them never stop.'

'Okay, okay. So why don't you go and ask him? Why don't you go over and say "Excuse me, I know I don't know your name, little Greek person, but are you waiting for me?" That should fetch a smile to his face. But remember, if you get arrested, we've only got traveller's cheques for bail.'

I stared at the man again. I was even more convinced it was him. I crossed the fifteen or so yards to the door. 'Excuse me.' In order to put him at his ease, I smiled my pleasant passport smile. 'I realize you don't know what I look like but are you waiting for me? . . . Harry Cole is my name.'

He never uttered a word, but instantly jumped into the sanctuary of the revolving doors and within seconds had twirled himself into the street.

I waited for the shrieks of delight to emerge from Joan and was rather surprised by their absence. On turning, I saw her deeply engaged in conversation with a genial-looking, slightly-built, middle-aged man. Could this be Bob? If so, where was the ladyfriend and how did he know Joan anyway? Then the thought struck me that perhaps it wasn't Bob. Was this possibly a foyer-frequenting dirty old man, or had my wife's luck changed? Perhaps any second she would follow my Greek friend through the still-rotating doors. Whatever the possibility, she appeared fascinated by him. Suddenly she looked up.

'Oh Harry, this is the gentleman you have been waiting for. May I introduce Bob's friend – Bill Fullilove. Not a Greek, you see.'

Bill turned, hand outstretched and a wide welcoming grin. 'Oh most definitely not a bleedin' Greek,' he confirmed, in as strong a south London accent as I have heard for years.

'No wonder I couldn't find you,' I said as he pumped my hand. 'I was looking for an American. I shouldn't think you've been here any longer than us.'

'Well, perhaps a little longer,' he differed.

'How little?' I persisted.

'Thirty years.'

'Thirty years! But you haven't a trace of the accent.'

'O'course not. I'm a Brit and proud of it. Anyway, what's all this about bleedin' Greeks?'

'It's too long a story. Come and have a drink.'

'But what about your friend Bob?' cut in Joan, whose teetotal reasoning is never as clear as abstainers would have us believe. 'He won't know where we are.'

'Oh, he'll know where we are right enough,' differed Bill gently. 'Think about it, love, where's the best place to overcome the shock of a thirty-two-year separation, if it ain't in a bar? You see, it's the first place any sensible bloke would look.' His logic impressed me. There is no doubt about it, I thought, I am really going to like this fellow. 'By the way,' he went on, 'I suppose I'm really responsible for this little get-together.'

'Are you?' she marvelled. 'But how? We've never met before.'

'Well, I was on one of my many trips back home, when I bought one of your husband's books about coppering in South London. I realized that the pair of them must have been at the same nick at the same time, so I lent Bob the book. That reminds me,' he said thoughtfully, 'the bugger never returned it.'

'Yes, but how did you meet Bob?' asked the puzzled

Joan, who loves these boring little human interest snippets.

'Staten Island Cricket Club,' he replied with a mischievous look, already sensing my curiosity would be unable to let that one pass.

'Staten Island Cricket Club?' I echoed. 'But Staten Island's in New York Harbour! Since when have they played cricket in New York? I thought their national game was rounders.'

'You'd better not let anyone hear you say that,' chuckled Bill. 'Baseball is a great religion here and they can get very, very touchy about it.'

'Which makes your cricket club even more of a surprise,' I persisted.

'Listen mate,' said the New York cockney. 'Expatriates both from England and the West Indies have been playing cricket on Staten Island since 1872. Even the great Don Bradman played there in 1932 – and he was out for a duck! There ain't many cricket clubs back home that can claim that, now is there?'

'Who got him out?' I sulked, 'Capone?'

Our move to the bar worked like a charm. Within seconds of reaching there, a transatlantic voice boomed across the room. 'That's just gotta be Harry Cole.' I was delighted on two counts. Obviously I was delighted to see Bob again after so long, but primarily because it bore out a long-held theory that one only meets the best people in pubs and bars.

Joan claims my reasoning is faulty. She says I keep meeting these people because of the life I have led and the company I have kept. She says if I did not go in so many bars, I would not meet so many people. Typical teetotal view, this. How many world problems have been solved on a twenty-mile walk? Precious few, I'll bet. Yet put me on a high stool, with a pint in my hand and a few amiable strangers around and I will give you international disarmament within twenty minutes.

'You dog!' said the voice. 'I'd know you anywhere. You haven't changed a scrap!'

Who is this fellow, I thought. Thirty-two years on and 'haven't changed a scrap'? I must have been the oldest, baldest, most wizened twenty-five-year-old in creation. I looked for the voice and I must say that its owner had certainly changed. When I had last seen him, he had been something of an athlete. Well, now he wasn't. A heavy, broad man with a wide, welcoming grin and a huge right hand that gripped mine like a bouncing vice. His lady-friend, Susan, also a Kentish expatriate, gave a warm smile of welcome and, to my relief, a much gentler handshake.

Thirty-two years is a long time to catch up, but the conversation flowed easily. Within minutes Bob revealed that he had left the London force for the Bermudan constabulary, and from there had moved on to small-time acting. He next worked as an agent to trace coats of arms for American families who felt the need for them (!), then bummed around the States in general before settling down as a civilian with the New York police department. Somewhere amongst that lot he had also been a tennis coach giving lessons to rich young wives.

'But I don't remember you playing tennis to that standard,' I queried.

'I never did,' he agreed. 'But a friend of mine did. He would give me a lesson in the morning and I would repeat the same lesson in the afternoon.'

'I think I've seen your protégées amongst the British

entries at Wimbledon,' said Joan. 'How about you, Bill?' she continued. 'I suppose you teach baseball?'

'Nah,' said the south Londoner, wrinkling his nose in disapproval. 'I came here temporarily thirty years ago. Now, two wives, two homes and three decades later, I'm still here temporarily.'

'He has Union Jack underpants,' explained Bob.

'So how do you two like New York?' asked the hitherto quiet Susan.

'Well, other than a few sights coming into town, you three are all we've seen. But as we are only here for two days, why don't we eat somewhere and you tell us about the place?'

'Fine. D'you have a place in mind?' asked Bob.

'No, that's where you three come in.'

'Well . . .' he said thoughtfully. 'The problem is, today is Labor Day.'

'I bet W.C. Fields never knew New York is as closed as Philadelphia,' I said.

'It's not,' he laughed. 'But many of the restaurants are.' He turned to Bill. 'As we arranged to take this pair out to dinner, d'you have any ideas, mate?'

'How about Smith and Wolanskys on Third Avenue? It apparently has something of a reputation and it's only two minutes' walk away.'

Smith and Wolanskys it was. Ten minutes later, we joined a small queue for a table at an apparently cult restaurant. There we were to have an indifferent meal, badly served, at an exorbitant price.

'I must tell you good folks,' said the brash young waiter as he presented a $161 bill to our hosts, for a small meal that did not include starters, dessert or wine: 'The check does not include service charge.'

'Well, doesn't that work out just fine,' replied Bill, 'because we didn't get any service.'

'No service and not much food,' mused Joan nostalgically. 'It's like being back in London.'

'If our prices were too much for you perhaps you should have tried the burger bar down the road.'

I sensed he had already said goodbye to his tip. (I was amazed to discover later that Bob still gave him a full ten per-cent!) I thought Bill best summed up our feelings when he wondered why it couldn't have been a civilized restaurant and closed like everywhere else.

One of the most difficult social tasks I know is to thank someone warmly for a lousy meal. I was also full of guilt for the price of the thing. We offered to return the compliment to our hosts the following evening. (Not at Smith and Wolanskys, mind.) Unfortunately Bob was the only one able to take up our offer.

'Before you go,' said Bill generously, 'how about a quick drive around Manhattan? I have my car here and traffic should have eased by now.'

We leaped at the offer and were soon marvelling at New York by night. Sadly, 'marvelling' was not always the correct word. Take Central Park, for instance.

'It really is a beautiful park,' praised Bob, 'but you'd have to be nuts to venture in there at this time of night.'

'Why?' asked Joan.

'Drugs, mainly. Pushers, fixers, addicts, muggers, and for variety, we even have the occasional murderer.'

'But this is your largest city park!'

'You don't have to tell me that. It stretches for more than fifty blocks.'

'So how can you put men into space and let the scum take over your central town park?'

'You think this is bad? Take a look at this street coming up soon.'

Within a few minutes, we drove along a widish thoroughfare that looked like a psychedelic interpretation of hell. Blatant prostitution was on offer, not only of both sexes but even some of indeterminate gender. No matter which way you looked at them, neither sex came readily to mind – some were almost beautiful (whatever they were), others were grotesque. Some were as feminine as Brando in a frock, other as masculine as Mother Teresa in diving boots. There were drug-peddlers by the dozen and porn movie houses everywhere. As our car slowed, several drug-pushers approached, assuming we were buyers.

'Look across the road,' said Bob, pointing through the window.

On the opposite side, and just able to thread their way through the throng of sellers, buyers, ponces and pimps, were two uniformed policemen. They appeared to see nothing of the mayhem of activity all around them.

'Why don't they do anything?' asked Susan, who seemed to be as puzzled by the scene as both Joan and I.

'Corruption.'

'Surely not!' I exploded disbelievingly. 'Never as obvious as that?'

'Oh no,' agreed Bob. 'Certainly not the corruption you are thinking about. This is almost a form of *inverse* corruption. This is the fear of having a corruption charge levelled against you. The result is what you see in front of you now.'

'You mean the uniform branch does nothing because of just the *threat* of a corruption allegation?'

'I mean just that. What you have to understand is, the morale of this force is rock-bottom. It couldn't be lower. You have politics in this force that you could never begin to understand in London. I feel so sorry for the men on the streets. They have no backing at all from their hierarchy.'

Within a few minutes of midnight we were back in front of our hotel.

'Well, thank you all,' I said gratefully, 'both for the drive and the commentary. I shall recommend to Cooks that they include it in all future tours.'

'But they will have to pay for the meal,' said Bill. 'After all, one can only have so much fun.'

We made our farewells and tottered our way through the revolving doors.

'I see your old pal is waiting for you,' said Joan wearily, as she nodded towards the corner of the foyer.

I glanced to my left. 'My old – ?' My question was cut short as an alarmed-looking middle-aged Greek made a beeline for the still-rotating doors.

On any morning of a package-tour, I wake (usually cockerel early) with my brain in neutral and my reasoning confused. It will take some seconds, probably minutes, to decipher exactly what city lies outside the window. The next trick is to remember the schedule for the day.

Our itinerary for the 6th of September read: 'Morning to mid-afternoon. Today we tour Manhattan. This includes visits to New York Harbour; Statue of Liberty; Greenwich Village; Chinatown; Wall Street; Italian Quarter; Central Park; The Hudson and East Rivers.' What it failed to mention was that one could easily spend all of that time (and more) simply queueing for the privilege of climbing the steps of the Statue of Liberty. The next note in the day's programme was almost certainly inserted by a sadist – and a female at that. It read: 'Rest of the day at leisure. This will doubtless provide the tourist with an invaluable opportunity for some exciting New York shopping.' Now there *is* a contradiction in terms! What cretin equates leisure with shopping? I bet it wasn't a man. Leisure is leisure. Shopping is purgatory. (This is the first lesson learned by every married man. Three months after our wedding, I accompanied Joan to D.H. Evans in Oxford Street to buy a coat – an operation that for myself takes about four minutes. After an hour and forty minutes, the assistant icily pointed out that 'We have over three thousand coats in this store but we obviously do not have one for modom' – and I could never have put it better!)

In any case, since when, pray, has any form of shopping been 'exciting'? The only exciting shopping I ever experienced was when I inadvertently (honest) staggered into the female changing-room in British Home Stores. I must be fair though, and say our day-tour certainly did include *all* of the above-mentioned locations. How much time we actually *spent* there, of course, was a very different proposition. Central Park was our record – I think we did it in a little under eight seconds.

'Don't forget what the courier said,' Joan reminded me.

'Er – hit me again with it,' I pleaded. 'I lost the drift of his thesis at the beginning of the third hour.'

She sighed. 'He said that even if we see nothing else, we must go to the top of the Empire State Building and see New York at dusk. Remember?'

'But we've seen everything else from ground level,' I pointed out wearily, 'so that excuses us, surely?'

'Oh come on,' she chided. 'We can't come all this way and not climb to the top of the Empire State, now can we? Even your old mate Kong made it to the top.'

'I know, and look what happened to him.' I was cheating a little by this attitude for I was equally intrigued by the idea.

'Well, you don't *have* to do it from the outside, of course. I understand they now have elevators. Why don't we pop up to the top, then phone Bob and take him for dinner?'

'You're on.'

I must confess I thought Joan was joking when she said it wasn't imperative to climb it from the outside. No doubt she was. But this was before we experienced the manners and attitudes of the attendants. I suppose it *was* about 7 p.m. and they *might* have had a long day. All I can say is, it showed. For some reason, passengers to the top of the building have to change escalators around the eightieth floor. It is a bit like changing trains really and provides you with the same uncertainty. You alight, not too sure if you have reached your destination, and promptly look for a friendly-faced uniform to reassure, or redirect, you. Well, you don't get it on the eightieth floor of the Empire State, I can tell you. They were about as friendly and helpful as the Death's Head Division of the Waffen S.S. 'NOT-THAT-GODDAMNED-LIFT-THAT-ONE! DON'T-YOU-UNDERSTAND-GODDAMNED-ENGLISH?' As three quarters of the passengers appeared Japanese, it was reasonable to assume they didn't.

'It appears statutory to sit an English exam before venturing to the top, honey,' said one of the few American voices in the escalator.

'I sure wish they'd told us before we paid our three bucks admission,' replied his female companion.

A minute or so later, all was more or less forgiven as we stepped on to the observation floor.

'God, but this is high!' marvelled Joan.

I made no reply. I assumed at that height she was talking to Him direct.

'Hey!' whispered Joan excitedly. 'Remember *On The Town*?'

'Of course. One of my all-time favourites.'

'Well, Gene Kelly, Sinatra and Betty Garrett danced on this very spot.'

'Don't forget Cyd Charisse,' I added nostalgically.

'Cyd Charisse? Cyd Charisse was never in *On The Town*.'

'Don't be silly. That was the only reason I saw it in the first place!'

The view had now become secondary.

'You know,' she said emphatically. 'I really do believe you're becoming senile. Just because you were in love with Cyd Charisse, you've gradually convinced yourself she was in every musical film you ever saw.'

'That's total nonsense – and in any case, I was never in love with Cyd Charisse. It was Ann Miller, if you must know. I have never told you before, but she was responsible for me not drinking tea in the army.'

'Why ever not?'

'Well, it was always said that they put bromide in the tea. It was supposed to . . . well, you know . . . slow you down, like.'

'But why did you want slowing down? You were in the army. I would have thought that the last thing the army would have wanted was slow soldiers.'

I looked about us. Others were becoming interested. I dropped my voice to little more than a whisper.

'Not *that* sort of slow. Bromide was supposed to stop you becoming sexually excited. The army wanted all your energy for itself, its thinking being, that the less energy we expended around suspender-tops and cleavages, the more we had for the assault course and rifle range.'

'So how does Ann Miller figure in all this?'

'I was frightened that if I drank too much tea, I would stop fancying her . . . I *was* very young at the time,' I pointed out.

'What a naïve little squaddie you were to be sure! And we've had to come three thousand miles to the top of the Empire State Building for me to find our your dark secret.'

I gestured around us. 'Well, you and about half the Japanese nation. Come on, I'm starving. Let's take Bob Woolley out for dinner.'

'Bromide free?'

'Bromide free.'

We reached ground level after being yelled at only twice and began to search for a taxi. I had assumed this would be easy; I had seen them enough in films. In fact in *On The Town* Betty Garrett had played the part of a cab-driver. Of course, we weren't actually expecting her, but it had never appeared too difficult to hire one. No matter if it had been an 'A' or 'B' picture, comedy or drama, rain or shine, the character would look up screen left and simply yell 'Taxi!' Sure enough, three seconds later, that flat yellow shape would roll slowly into view. First lesson – do not believe all you see in the cinema!

Now it is not as if there are no cabs; New York is infested with them. Some are full, others empty, but most of them give the impression that hiring is just about the last thing in which they are interested. Their prime function seems to be that of an outnumbered fighter-plane in World War Two. They tear kamikaze-like into the mass of other traffic, weaving in and out continuously. I never actually saw one dive and climb but all I can say is, I expected to. I felt I was watching a re-run of the Battle of Britain. Traffic signals are an irrelevance. So too, I discovered, is the English language. It may not be that they deliberately ignore the signals, so much as that they are unable to read them in the first place. God knows how they would make out on the elevators of the Empire State Building. One frustrated New Yorker later assured me they saw themselves not so much as cabbies, more as freedom fighters, trail-blazing a path across their alien-held homeland. This theory is probably correct – so few seem to speak English that no doubt the rest of the city's population must seem foreign to them.

In London, a cab-driver spends about two years learning 'The Knowledge'. At the end of that time, they will be expected to know every street, alley, hotel and theatre in central London. In New York, I believe it is the passenger who acquires 'The Knowledge', because cab-drivers hardly know their way home. In London cabbies are experts on any subject you care to mention. If they know you are a writer, then every one of them will be a novelist. If you paint, they are all artists. If you are visiting someone in hospital, you can bet your driver will have just recovered from an operation so mindblowingly complex that medical science is still stunned by its sheer magnitude. In short, they talk. In fact, like Greeks, they rarely stop.

In New York, on the other hand, the only English your

cabbie will utter is when he tells you how much you owe him. This makes life particularly difficult when you do not know the Iranian for 'I-think-we-came-the-long-way-round-and-you've-overcharged-me-by-six-dollars.'

Twenty minutes later, we finally nailed a cab. I handed the driver a now-crumpled note of Bob's address. Needless to say, he was not Betty Garrett.

Of course, handing over a written note is one thing, his understanding it is very much another. He shook his head. 'Nix,' he replied.

'What's that mean?' asked Joan curiously.

I shrugged. 'If it's not Bolivian for something rude, it might be that he's simply telling us that he can't read English.'

'So what do we do now?'

'Well, he may not be able to read but hopefully he's not deaf. I'll try telling him. Sec . . . ond . . . Aven . . . nue . . . yes?' I slowly explained, raising two fingers.

'I wouldn't raise those fingers quite so much if I was you,' said Joan helpfully. 'Why don't you give him the other half of the address?'

'Because Second Avenue is *not* the actual place. The address we want is Lafayette Street and Houston.'

'Then why are you telling him Second Avenue?'

'Because Bob said that was the best way to go.'

'Don't you think it's complicated enough without you giving him route directions as well? He *is* a cabbie after all. Let *him* find the best way.'

'I just thought if I said Second Avenue convincingly, he would think I knew my way around New York and he wouldn't be so likely to overcharge. That's all.'

The cabbie turned and with an accent even I knew was

pure New York drawled, 'Second Avenue is der pits for traffic. But if dat's watcha want, dat's watcha gonna get.'

I was by now hopelessly embarrassed. 'I'm sorry,' I blurted. 'Look, er, we'll leave it to you, eh? Go another way if it suits you.'

'I can't go anudder way,' he snapped.

'Why?'

'Second Avenue's der only way I know.'

We decided we were now well out of our depth and silently completed the rest of the journey by staring out of opposite windows. Our cabbie was certainly right about one thing. Second Avenue *was* 'der pits for traffic'. Even so, we finally reached our destination just minutes late. Bob's time was limited because he was at work and had taken an extended meal break, and our late arrival had done little to help his time-table.

'We'll need to go to a local restaurant I'm afraid.' he said. 'I don't have time enough to travel. D'you like Italian?'

'We love Italian.'

'Good, Little Italy is nearby. I know a place that should be suitable.'

Well, he was certainly right about that; it was the sort of Italian restaurant they don't even have in Italy. It was straight out of every Capone film I ever saw, a small family place of about a dozen or so tables that only lacked Edward G. Robinson, George Raft and the Mafia – even the local priest ate there.

'He doesn't look much like Pat O'Brien,' whispered Joan with a hint of disappointment in her voice.

'Who's Pat O'Brien?' asked Bob.

'We keep forgetting, you're one of the younger set, aren't you. Pat O'Brien always seemed to be the priest in gangster movies,' I explained. 'At the end of the film he would usually escort James Cagney to the electric chair.'

'Why?' persisted Bob.

'What are friends for?' asked Joan.

The meal was, of course, excellent, and my embarrassment for the previous night was not eased when I collected the bill. Three meals, beer and wine – twenty-seven dollars! We said our farewells to Bob and under his expert tutelage, managed to catch the seventh empty taxi that tried to drive by.

'Lexington and East Forty-eighth please,' I instructed.

'Eh?' frowned the driver.

'Lex . . . ing . . . ton . . . and . . . East . . . For . . . ty . . . eighth,' I repeated laboriously.

'I think he would have been happier if you had said Rangoon,' whispered Joan.

'Well, you watch the meter in case he charges us for it,' I replied anxiously.

For the entire journey back to our hotel, he drove with one hand on the steering wheel and the other clutching the car microphone, which was never more than half an inch from his large, slack lips. Into this he poured a torrent of non-stop verbal that sounded like a political speech in Urdu. Three violated traffic-lights, two wrong-way streets and one banned 'U' turn later, we were deposited, to our grateful surprise, outside the Lexington. It was there we realized that 'Eh?' was obviously the only English he knew, for he repeated it twice more when I gave him the tip.

We had glided through the revolving doors and were crossing the thickly-carpeted foyer. I was just subjecting my brain to its usual hotel reception battering (i.e. Now what the hell is our room number?) when Joan sidled up with a blatantly mischievous tone in her voice.

'I don't want to worry you, particularly after such a pleasant evening, but guess who is standing behind us in the corner of the foyer?'

I refused to look. Although I did notice the gentle swish of the revolving doors suddenly increase to a deep rumble . . .